Carbon Shinai
カーボンシナイ

CF-Type
DB-Type
K1-Type
K2-Type

We have improved the official Carbon Shinai rubber stopper.
Orange | Red | Yellow
The NEW official rubber stopper.
¥300 (domestic Japanese price)

WARNING!!
Never use anything other than our official rubber stopper on your Carbon Shinai !!

When using your Carbon Shinai.....

1. To prevent injury, please use our official rubber stopper. Do not use stoppers made for conventional bamboo shinai on your Carbon Shinai, as there is a risk of injury to your opponent if the tip breaks through and enters their men grill.

2. When choosing a sakigawa (leather tip), make sure that it is more than 5cm in length and completely covers our rubber stopper. If the sakigawa is shorter than 5cm, there is a risk of injury to your opponent if a slat slips out and enters their men grill.

3. Do not shave the plastic surface of your Carbon Shinai. If you shave the surface, the black carbon fiber will be exposed, causing damage that may result in injury to your opponent.

4. Always check the condition of the surface of your Carbon Shinai before and during use. As soon as you notice any cracks, or peeling of the surface, or if black carbon fiber is exposed on any part of the outside, inside or edges of the Shinai, or you notice any other damage, stop using the shinai immediately. There is a danger of injury to your opponent if your Carbon Shinai is split or broken.

5. When tying the nakayui (leather binding), either tie a knot in the tsuru-ito (cord), or tie one end of the nakayui to the tsuru-ito, or by another means ensuring that is does not move up and down during use. If there is any damage whatsoever to the sakigawa, tsukagawa (hilt), rubber stopper, tsuru-ito and so on, replace them immediately.

6. If the tip of the Carbon Shinai is damaged, or a slat is protuding out of the sakigawa, there is a danger that it could enter your opponent's men grill and injure them.

Kendogu Revolution

Mu-Jun Men
武楯面

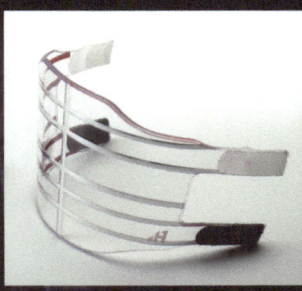

SG-Type

WARNING!!

1. Under no circumstances should organic solvents (such as thinner, alcohol, benzene, toluene, acetone, gasoline, kerosene, etc.), acidic or alkali chemicals, domestic cleansers, car cleansers, or anti-mist sprays, be used to clean the shield. These substances will cause the shield to deteriorate, leading to clouding, cracking or breaking, thereby resulting in danger of injury to the face.

2. Should the shield develop deep scratches or cracks on either the outer or inner surface, discontinue use of the shield immediately, and replace it with an undamaged shield. If the shield is used in such a condition, there is a danger of it breaking, causing injury to the face.

3. It should be fully understood that, as with the traditional Japanese Kendo-Men (mask), there is still the danger of injury to the face through fragments of broken bamboo or Carbon Shinai pieces penetrating through areas not covered by the shield.

- SCIENCE TO SEEK SAFETY -
HASEGAWA
HASEGAWA CORPORATION

WEB : http://kendo.hasegawakagaku.co.jp/
Email : contact@hasegawakagaku.co.jp

Carbon Shinai — Points to be checked

DANGER !! **ATTENTION !!**

Before these happen.....

Although the Carbon Shinai is much more durable than a conventional bamboo one, it will inevitably become damaged since it is a sword that is used to repeatedly strike and thrust your opponent. Therefore, inspect the condition of the surface, sides or reverse of the Carbon Shinai's slats before, during and after use, and stop using it immediately should damage like in the following pictures be observed. (These pictures are just a few examples of many.)

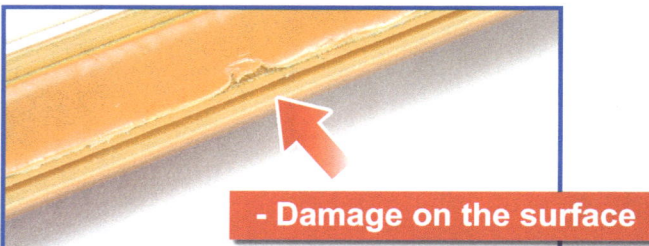

- Damage on the surface

- An unglued surface sheet

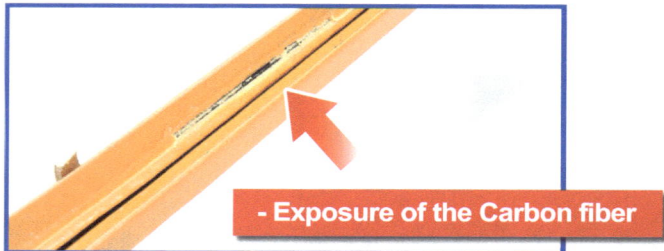

- Exposure of the Carbon fiber

- Longitudinal crack on the surface

- Damage and ungluing of the surface

There is the case where the reverse gets cracked even without any damage on the surface. Inspect the inside of the Shinai by pushing the pieces with the fingers and unbinding the Naka-yui.

- Crack on the reverse

HASEGAWA-KOTE

- Detachable and washable "Tenouchi" is easy to wash and dry.

- "Tenouchi" is replaceable when torn. No need to repair.

Kote (Main part)

Tenouchi (Inner)

- SCIENCE TO SEEK SAFETY -

HASEGAWA CORPORATION
http://kendo.hasegawakagaku.co.jp/

KENDO WORLD Volume 7.4 June 2015 Contents

Editorial — 2

The 16th WKC — 4

Reflections on the Women's Competition at the 16th World Kendo Championships — 24

Kendo Wa: A Film Series About World Kendo — 27

Kendo for Adults — 30

Obituary—Inoue Yoshihiko 1928–2015 — 35

sWords of Wisdom
"Yōi wo katarazu" — 36

Reidan-jichi Part 19 Waza Basics — 38

Big Time Grading Pointers — 40

Obituary—Mochizuki Teruo 1945–2015 — 42

Walking in the Footsteps of "The Exceptional Charles Boxer" — 43

Bujutsu Jargon Part 7 — 46

Hagakure and "Sutemi" — 48

Swords and Teapots
The Remarkable Story of Chūjō Kageaki — 52

Obituary—Terry Holt 1939–2015 — 53

Book Review
Miyamoto Musashi—A Life in Arms — 54

Arming the kids — 56

Martial Aids
The Shogun Traveller Bag™ by Shogun Kendogu — 58

Tea and the Kenshi
Sadō, the Way of Tea, and Kendo, the Way of the Sword. — 60

Book Review
Chinese Martial Arts from Antiquity to the Twenty-First Century — 64

The Ninja & The Sword — 66

Shinai Sagas
Once Upon a Time in Japantown — 69

Musō Jikiden Eishin-ryū Riai
The Meaning of the Kata: Part 2 — 74

Book Review
Encyclopedia of Japanese Martial Arts — 86

Thoughts on Monouchi and Datotsu-bu — 87

Does the Time of the Attacking Action in KENDO Influence the Success Rate of IPPON? — 92

Kendo World Staff
- Bunkasha International President & Editor-in-Chief— Alex Bennett PhD
- Bunkasha International Vice President & Assistant Editor—Michael Ishimatsu-Prime MA
- Bunkasha International Vice President & Graphic Design—Shishikura 'Kan' Masashi
- Bunkasha International Vice President—Hamish Robison
- Bunkasha International Vice President—Michael Komoto MA
- Bunkasha International General Manager—Baptiste Tavernier MA
- Senior Consultants—Yonemoto Masayuki, Shima Masahiko

KW Staff Writers / Translators / Photographers / Graphic Designer / Sub-editors
- Axel Pilgrim PhD
- Blake Bennett MA
- Bruce Flanagan MA
- Bryan Peterson
- Charlie Kondek
- Gabriel Weitzner
- Honda Sōtarō PhD
- Irnafuji Masahiro MBA
- Jeff Broderick
- Kate Sylvester MA
- Sergio Boffa PhD
- Stephen Nagy PhD
- Steven Harwood MA
- Stuart Gibson
- Taylor Winter
- Tony Cundy
- Trevor Jones
- Tyler Rothmar
- Yamaguchi Remi
- Vivian Yung
- Yulin Zhuang

KW would like to thank the following people and organisations for their valuable cooperation:
- All Japan Kendo Federation
- Hasegawa Teiichi - President, Hasegawa Corporation
- Kendo Jidai Magazine
- Kendo Nihon Magazine
- Nippon Budokan Foundation
- Shogun Kendogu
- TOZANDO

Guest Writers
- Antony Cummins (Historical Ninjutsu Research Team)
- Geoff Salmon (Kendo Kyōshi 7-dan, Mumeishi Kendo Club, London)
- Graham Sayer (Kendo Renshi 7-dan, NZ Kendo Federation)
- Hatano Toshio (Kendo Kyōshi 8-dan)
- Iwatate Saburō (Kendo Hanshi 8-dan)
- James Gordon Ogle (Cardiff Metropolitan University)
- Kate Sylvester (Victoria University)
- Kenneth Reed (Omotosenke School of Tea)
- Kim Taylor (Iaido 7-dan, sdksupplies.com)
- Ōya Minoru (Prof. International Budo University; Kendo Kyōshi 7-dan)
- Paul Budden (Kendo Kyōshi 7-dan, Kodokan Kendo U.K.)

COPYRIGHT 2015 Bunkasha International Corporation. No part of this publication may be reproduced in any form whatsoever without written permission from the publisher, except by writers who are permitted to quote brief passages for the purpose of review or reference. Kindly contact Bunkasha International Corporation at info@kendo-world.com.

Editorial Conventions Used in KW Inevitably in a magazine of this nature, many non-English words appear in the text. All Japanese words are italicised and include macrons (ū, ō) etc., apart from common place names and nouns, and words in some captions and headings. As a general exception, KW treats all the martial arts (budo), such as kendo, iaido, jodo, ranks, and so on as Anglicised words without using macrons. Japanese names are written in accordance to the traditional Japanese manner of family name followed by given name. Traditional ryūha are written with capitals and therefore are not italicised. 'Kata' with a capital 'K' refers to the set of Nippon Kendo Kata, and kata refers to set forms in general. The masculine personal pronoun is used throughout the text in some articles in the interest of readability, and is in no way meant to slight the significant contributions made by female kendoka.

Editorial
Reflections on three big days

By Alex Bennett

The 16WKC finished with a bang. In the end, Japan came first in all of the competitions, but jeepers it was close. Being the first WKC decided through a bid system, this tournament was special in many ways. The fact that it was held in the Nippon Budokan, the venue for the 1st WKC held 45 years earlier, made it just that little bit more exceptional. But not only that, it was the biggest tournament ever with over 600 participants representing 56 countries and regions in attendance. The venue was even graced by the presence of Princess Yoko. She attended as a royal guest on the first day, and then incognito the following days. As a kendoka herself, she seemed to be much more comfortable in the bleachers than the royal box seat.

With a capacity crowd of over 10,000 on the last day, I would guess that it was the best attended WKC ever. It really did have a colosseum feel with spectators packed right up in the nosebleed seats looking down on the fierce duels taking place below. Also, this was the first time the matches were televised live on NHK, enabling tens, if not hundreds of thousands more people to watch the event as it unfolded.

With the record number of participants, spare a thought for the beleaguered *shinpan*. Matches started at 9:00am and continued well into the evening three days running. With only four *shiai-jo* and 36 *shinpan*, it was a full time job without respite in what was quite an inhospitable environment. It was hot, muggy, crowded, with TV cameras everywhere, and even a rather significant earthquake thrown in for good measure. Actually, the magnitude 8.5 quake struck on Saturday night right in the middle of the awards ceremony for the women's competition. I thought, if Japan had lost that day, then the timing of the shake would really have been something [for the Japanese media] to write about. "Divine retribution" and all that carry on.

Well done to Hayashi Tatsuo-sensei who reacted with such speed and composure that he must have known a quake was imminent. His well-rehearsed emergency announcements kept the startled competitors reassured, and they were terribly relieved and grateful when he guided everybody from underneath the colossal speakers swinging ominously overhead. Being a seismically active country, the Japanese were fairly relaxed about the shaking and knew that the Budokan was not going to collapse around their ears. But tell that to some of the terrified participants who have never experienced a violent tremor before.

Back to the *shinpan*. One can only imagine the physical and mental fatigue when the finals were reached each day. Imagine again, what it must have been like by the third day. With the record number of competitors and teams, the host federation knew that the scheduling would be tight. It was proposed by the AJKF that the preliminary heats be done away with, and the knockout tournament system be employed from the outset. The FIK directors vetoed this proposal, and I am sure it would have been highly unpopular if it had passed. It is a long and expensive journey to Japan if you get knocked out in your first match!

The pools remained in the end, but there were suggestions of making the preliminary matches shorter in duration, or even increasing the number of *shiai-jō* in the early rounds and utilising the dozens of highly skilled local 8-dan as *shinpan* to take the load off the FIK *shinpan* delegation. These ideas, however, were not approved by the AJKF as options for discussion, and so it came to pass that the original FIK *shinpan* had to endure three consecutive *shinpan*-ing marathons. Was that fair on them or the competitors? Perhaps this WKC was unique in terms of scale, but I can't help thinking that a little more flexibility to meet the special circumstances would have been justified.

One thing that stood out about this WKC was the time that many teams spent in Japan beforehand. The fact that the event was held in the spiritual home of kendo gave hundreds of dedicated kenshi and their supporters a rare opportunity/excuse to make a pilgrimage here. All federations around the world have, over the years, cemented tight bonds of friendship with individual Japanese teachers, clubs or regions. Evidently delegations were quick to make use of these ties to prepare for the *shiai*, and also enjoy the Japanese experience. The hosts were also eager to give their visitors plenty of fond memories to take back with them. Regional NHK television stations were having a field day with heart-warming human interest kendo stories with a lot more spice than the local flower show, or as a counterbalance to pressing news like the death of Tama the cat! I kid you not.

I know that the Italian team, for example, prepared under the watchful eyes of top ranked Shizuoka teachers. The Americans, Thais, and three other teams sweated it out in the final build up with the students at the University of Tsukuba, home to Takenouchi Yūya. The New Zealand team spent the best part of 3 weeks of intensive preparation at my workplace, Kansai University, and in places such as Minoh City where team members have a special relationship. Having a foot on each side of the fence, I could see firsthand how the experience was a stimulating eye opener for some of the junior members of the NZ team, as well as for the Japanese students who were suddenly inundated with a bunch of gangly, mean looking foreigners.

It made me reflect on the ideal of *kōken-chiai*, or to learn respect through crossing swords through traipsing the same long, hard, laborious path. Of course, making a mark on the world stage at the WKC is everybody's primary objective, or dream. But when it is all said and done, it is a chance where thousands of people can come together with a common passion. The level of world kendo for both men and women is undoubtedly improving with each WKC that goes by. I have also noticed how the bonds of international friendship continue to evolve and strengthen over time—surely a wonderful aspect of kendo that we should cherish.

On that note, Kendo World opened a shop at the Budokan, and it was fantastic to have so many people dropping by to say hi. In the days leading up to the WKC, the KW team spent many sleepless nights preparing a special edition magazine for the event. We covered the history of all the world championships to date, plus plenty of other relevant information. The special edition was sold at our store along with our own KW brand *kote*, and other kendo goodies. If you weren't in Tokyo for the big event, you can still purchase these items on the KW website. With all the kendo equipment on sale throughout the narrow Budokan corridors, hundreds of hardened kenshi looked like kids in the proverbial candy store, thoroughly enjoying the experience from so many different angles.

Alas, now it's back to the mundane world. I was involved with the 16th WKC with three hats on this time: NZ Kantoku, AJKF International Committee, and of course Kendo World. There was never a dull moment in any of these operations, and life went into suspended animation for approximately a month. I am suffering for my habit now with a seemingly insurmountable pile of work to chip away at, as I'm sure many others are, too. It all seems like a dream now, but a damn good one.

Now we look forward to three more years of build up for the next congregation of the world's kenshi in Korea. I reckon that'll be a cracker too. I can't help but wonder if there will be murmurs from the ranks about introducing recourse to video *shinpan* in the case of controversy, as has been tested in corporate competitions in Korea. But, let's burn that bridge later.

The 16th WKC

At the International Kendo Federation (FIK) general assembly that was held during the 15th WKC in Novara, Italy, in 2012, Japan was awarded the right to host the 16th World Kendo Championships in 2015. After waiting three years for what was surely the most eagerly anticipated kendo event in history, the 16th World Kendo Championships were convened from Friday May 29 to Sunday May 31, 2015. For the first time since the inaugural WKC in 1970, it was held at the *Nippon Budokan*. This was the fourth time that Japan hosted the WKC; the other two occasions being the 4th (1979, Sapporo) and the 10th (1997, Kyoto) WKCs.

The 16th WKC was by far the biggest to date, and all but one of the 57 FIK registered federations attended this championship. There were 52 and 34 teams in the men's and women's team competition, respectively, while the men's individual competition saw 209 competitors take the floor at the Budokan on May 29. A total of 154 women competed in the individual championships on Saturday May 30 before the women's team competition.

Proving the continued popularisation and dissemination of kendo throughout the world, the 16th WKC also witnessed the debut of five federations: Croatia, Indonesia, Mongolia, Slovenia, and Turkey. These federations have been around for a few years: Croatia's was founded in 2004, Mongolia's in 1999, and Slovenia's in 2000. Turkey's first kendo clubs started in 1999.

The Indonesia Kendo Association was only formed in 2010, but kendo has been present there for more than ten years, with clubs in six major cities.

Kendo World spoke with Indonesia Kendo Association President Marcel Oesman just three days after his association joined the FIK. He said: "We are very grateful for this opportunity. I feel we have a lot to learn and a lot to do, and I hope we will be a good member of the FIK. On the side of our members, I hope that joining the FIK will help to improve both the quantity and quality of Indonesia's kendo."

By Michael Ishimatsu-Prime and Tyler Rothmar

Oesman was positive about his country's debut at the WKC, noting that while this was the highest-level tournament his association had attended to date, Indonesian competitors were able to win some matches before being knocked out. "It's not disappointing, it's encouraging," he said, adding, "It gave us a clearer direction about what we have to do to improve our kendo. I'm very impressed by the level of kendo of countries we've never met before, such as from the Americas and Europe. Japan as well, of course, as well as other strong Asian countries. Within Indonesia, the number one challenge that I feel we have is, as a third-world country, we have different economic levels between our cities. So it's difficult for the standard or level of economic development to be even. Income per capita versus the cost of equipment and travelling is a bit difficult to manage, especially for young people who are students or just starting a career. But I am feeling positive."

At the 15th WKC in Novara, there were some issues with the behaviour of the crowd, specifically during the men's team competition final. Some of the refereeing decisions were met with booing from the crowd, and the etiquette displayed by some of the competitors left a lot to be desired. During the 16th WKC, on occasion it was easy to understand if the crowd was unhappy with the judgements, but there was no repeat of the events of three years ago, from the competitors either. It was a very good-spirited WKC, maybe because it was in the spiritual home of kendo, and what a fantastic venue it was.

Over the three days, a total of 22,593 spectators visited the N*ippon* Budokan, with the largest crowd of 10,287 visiting on the final day for the men's team competition. Throughout the WKC, the crowd showed their pleasure when any of the Japanese or Korean *kenshi* conceded a point or lost. This was most likely not through any particular disdain for either of those countries, but probably because it was a shock, and maybe because it represents a small step in the right direction. However, as will be explained in the following sections, this did not happen often.

The 16th WKC

The Men's Individual Competition

The men's individual competition kicked off on Friday, May 29. The preliminary round consisted of 67 three-man and five two-man leagues; the winner of each league progressed to the knockout rounds.

Of the five debut federations in this WKC, only Slovenia did not compete in the men's individuals. Despite their inexperience at this level of competition, a competitor from each of Croatia, Indonesia, Mongolia, and Turkey progressed to the knockout competition. Mongolian Urtnasan Erdenebileg was defeated by two *men* strikes from Japan's Murase Ryo. Erdenebileg matched Murase for physicality, and had a slight height advantage, but in the end it was the latter's superior speed and timing that got him through that round. Despite Borna Ban (Croatia) making a promising start against Ireland's Lee Cahill with a *kote* strike after about 2m30s, which came after a period of slightly more pressure and attempted *ippon* than his Irish opponent, Ban conceded two *men* strikes. The first was a *hiki-men* in response to his own attempted *men* strike, and the next came very soon after the restart. Turkey's Can Aydogdu was beaten by eventual best-8 finisher Krzysztof Bosak of Poland by a solitary *men* strike a little under a minute into the encounter. Indonesia's Pandu Tresnalaga was undone by a *men-kaeshi-dō* and a *de-gote* from Jouke van der Woude (Netherlands), who finished in the best-16.

Even though these debutants went out in the first round of the knockout stage, their performance must surely give confidence and hope to the other members of their federations that their training is going in the right direction. The future certainly looks bright for them.

The greatest upset of the day was Bosak's defeat of H-G. Sung of Korea in the second round. Sung took *men* soon after the start. After a brief delay for Sung to change his *shinai*, the match restarted. Winning by one *ippon*, it appeared that Sung was not separating from *tsubazeriai* quickly enough and was then given a *hansoku*. Sung then had to be more assertive to avoid a second *hansoku*, and as he made an effort to strike *men*, Bosak equalised with a *degote* that sent the crowd wild. Following that *ippon*, Bosak appeared not to be separating and was then given a *hansoku*, which was surprising, as time was running out. However, straight after the restart, Bosak closed in on Sung, who raised his *shinai* defensively. Bosak still went for *men* and scored.

The real star of the day, however, was Takenouchi Yuya, the current and youngest ever All Japan Champion. As a fourth-year university student, he was competing in what will surely be the first of many WKC. In the league stage, he defeated Garrett Matsumoto (Hawaii) with a *hiki-men* and *men*, but it could have been over sooner as on two occasions he garnered one flag. His next league match was against Alex Dubrowskis-Renner (Latvia). He took *men*

The Men's Individual Competition Result

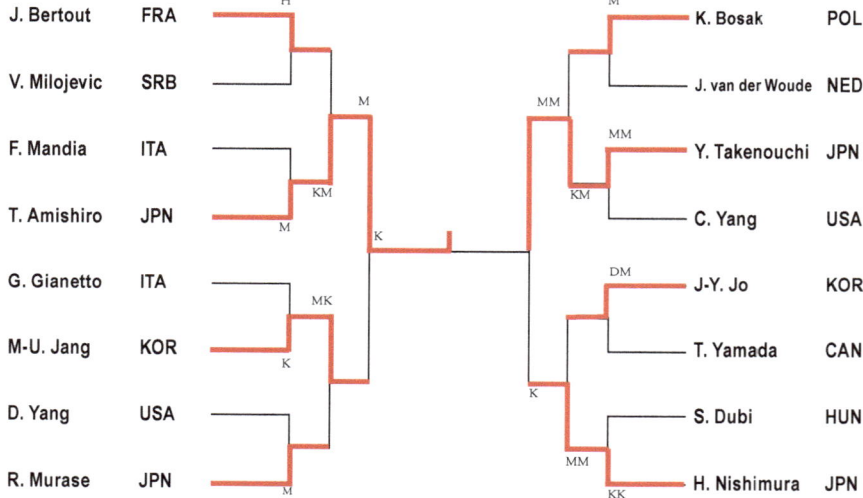

with his first attempt, and then *kote*, ending the match in under 20 seconds. In the second round, he faced Dario Baeli (Italy) and won with a *hiki-men* and *men*. Against Sweden's Jimmy Cedervall he scored a straight *kihon kote*, and sealed it with a *men*.

It was then into the best-16 round, in which all four of the Japanese men were present. However, only two of the Koreans (M-U. Jang and J-Y. Jo) and two of the Americans (the Yang brothers) made it to this stage. Surprisingly, none of the Brazilians or Canadians, who are usually fixtures at this stage, made it this far. Seven of the final 16 came from Europe, up one from the previous WKC.

Here, Takenouchi faced Chris Yang (USA) for his toughest match so far. However, after about 1m30s, he

moved in, dropping the tip of his *shinai* to open his *kote*. Yang took the bait, but Takenouchi was ready and took *men*. Chances were few and far between for Takenouchi as Yang was making it very difficult for him to get into his rhythm. Despite this, it was another *hiki-men* from Takenouchi that ended the match.

Then into the quarterfinal round, Europe had its joint best-ever showing at the WKC with two competitors: Jonathan Bertout (France) and Bosak (Poland). Bertout also made it to this stage at the 15th WKC together with Belgium's Caroll Tange. A European has yet to make it into the best-4, but surely that is becoming more and more of a possibility as the years pass.

At this stage, Bosak met Takenouchi. Again it was

Takenouchi's *hiki-men* that got the first *ippon* and he then progressed to the next round with a *kote*.

In the semifinal, Takenouchi came face-to-face with Nishimura. These two also met in the quarterfinal of the AJKC in 2014. Takenouchi won that match with a single *men* strike. Nishimura had the tougher run to this stage, defeating Omasa (Brazil), S. Dubi (Hungary) and then Korea's J-Y. Jo. Despite this, the advantage was to be his. In a little under 30s, Takenouchi found himself in unfamiliar territory as Nishimura exploded forward to take a lighting quick *kote*. Takenouchi was not afforded as much time as in some of his earlier matches and had to be vigilant. Nishimura had a good attempt at *hiki-men* soon after the restart but nothing was given. About 30s later Takenouchi evened the score with a men. From *tsubazeriai*, as Takenouchi and Nishimura were separating, they both stopped retreating. Takenouchi quickly pushed down on Nishimura's *shinai* and went for men and scored. That was his tenth *men* strike in seven matches. His other two *ippon* were *kote*.

He advanced to the final, where he would meet Amishiro Tadakatsu (Japan). Amishiro is a policeman in Hyogo prefecture and is more than ten years Takenouchi's senior. Hugely experienced, he has placed third in the AJKC and has won the police individual competition. He certainly had a difficult route to the final and had to defeat Korea's B-H. Park in the second round, Brandon Harada (USA) in the third round, then Fabrizio Mandia (Italy), then France's Bertout, and the giant M-U. Jang (Korea) before facing the current All Japan Champion in the final.

Takenouchi had the first attack of any substance, a *kote*, very early on, but for the next few minutes it was very cagey with both knowing what was at stake. Takenouchi tried to unleash his *hiki-men*, which had been so effective, but it looked like Amishiro was wise to that. For the first time Takenouchi went into *enchō*; Amishiro for the second. Just five seconds in, Takenouchi tried to lure in Amishiro to strike his *kote* so that he could do *kote-kaeshi-men*, but Amishiro was just too quick and became the sixteenth world champion, winning with a *kote* strike.

The Women's Individual Competition

The women's individual competition started the second day of the 16th WKC. As usual, the Japanese women were the favourites with the Koreans next. Much like the men, Japan's women have won every title since the women's competition started. When compared to their male compatriots, they have actually been more dominant as they have taken the top two places in every WKC. In fact, only once has a non-Japanese competitor broken into the top four: Eliete Takashina (Brazil) finished third at the 14th WKC. However, Takashina would not get the chance to repeat her heroics as she was only competing in the team competition on this occasion.

Of the five debut nations, only Indonesia, Slovenia and Turkey entered the women's individual championships. Actually, Slovenia's only competitors were two women. Usually, it is women who are lacking in the delegations. Andorra, Croatia, Denmark, Dominican Republic, Latvia, Luxembourg, Montenegro, and Portugal had no female competitors. Some of the other nations—Argentina, Bulgaria, Czech Republic, Greece, Hungary, Ireland, Israel, Lithuania, New Zealand, Russian Federation, Serbia, South Africa, and Venezuela—only entered women into the individual competition. Hopefully, in future WKCs we will be able to see equal participation for both men and women.

Much like male competitors from the debut federations, women from Slovenia and Turkey qualified for the knockout rounds. In the first round, Slovenia's Tanja Greif met Sayo van der Woude (Netherlands). About fifty seconds in, van der Woude lured Greif into making an attack and scored a great *men-nuki-dō*. Soon after, following a flurry of strikes, van der Woude sealed it with a *kote* strike. Turkey's Busra Aydogdu faced off against Japan's Tayama Akie. Tayama scored with a textbook *hiki-dō* from *tsubazeriai*, and quickly followed that with a *hiki-kote*. And again, like the men, advancing to the tournament stage in your federation's first WKC should been seen as a positive result.

Japan and Korea were predictably dominant in the league stage with none of their competitors conceding an *ippon*. Most of their matches were won by two *ippon*, but on four occasions the Koreans won by only one. Tayama, a former All Japan Champion, had a bit of a rough ride against the 16-year-old American, Yuri Kil. Tayama was about a head taller and nine years older than her opponent, but Kil certainly took the fight to her. Early on in the match, Kil had one flag raised for a *kote*, and was certainly matching her opponent for aggression. It took about 2m20s for Tayama to finally score—a *men*—but could not get the second and the match went the distance. In her other league match, Kil took a little over a minute to defeat Brazil's Vivian Omasa. Despite going out at the league stage after Tayama defeated Omasa, Kil will definitely be one to watch for the future.

Another young American to watch out for is 17-year-old Esther Kim. In the league stage, she defeated Mexico's Melisa Martinez and Carolina Salgado (Chile). Then in the first-round of the knockout stage against Konstantina Charmpali (Greece), her first attack, a strike to *kote*, got one flag raised. She then scored with a great *men* after Charmpali's failed *hiki-men*. Kim then scored with a *hiki-men* very soon after the restart, finishing the match in under a minute.

In the second round, Kim then faced Japan's Matsumoto Mizuki, a fourth-year university student at Hosei University. Matsumoto was runner-up in the All Japans, won both the team and individual university student championships, as well as team and individual high school championships. She is clearly a competitor with a strong pedigree, and only 22. Kim made a great account of herself, but Matsumoto was just too strong and won with a *kote* and fantastic *men* strike.

Unlike in the men's individual competition, Europe was not particularly well represented in the women's best-16. There were three women to the men's seven. Hungary's Marina Boviz came through the league stage by beating China's Mingrui Zhao with a *men-kaeshi-dō* and a *men*, and then defeated Marianne Skiftesvik (Norway) with a two *kote* strikes. In the first round of the knockout stage, she faced Hawaii's Erika Hill who was a sterner test than her previous matches. Still, Boviz managed to grind out a win with a solitary *men* strike. In the second round, she fought South Africa's Carle Joubert who she defeated with *men* strike in *enchō*. The third round (best-16) encounter was against one of Europe's strongest female competitors, Sayo van der Woude, a student at the International Budo University in Chiba, Japan, and who was in her second consecutive best-16 at the WKC.

In the league stage, against Argentina's Carolina Cavallera van der Woude took *men* after about seven seconds and then ended the match about 15 seconds later with a *kote* strike. In van der Woude's other league match against Brazil's Grace Ito, she took *men* but then conceded *men* very soon after. The match was decided in *enchō* when van der Woude scored a great *kote*.

But back to the third round and the van der Woude versus Boviz match. This was a much closer match than either of them had had before. With about three-quarters of the match gone, Boviz scored *kote*. Time was running out so van der Woude had to get the *ippon* to stay in it. She went on the attack as Boviz seemed to be content to soak up the pressure. However, van der Woude got the *ippon* she needed, a *dō* strike. No sooner had the referee said "*hajime*" to restart the match, the buzzer sounded to signal the end of regulation time. Great timing. What followed was several minutes of *enchō* during which van der Woude was given a *hansoku*, presumably for too much time in *tsubazeriai*. In the end, van der Woude sealed it with a *dō* strike to progress to the quarterfinal and a meeting with the aforementioned Japanese, Matsumoto Mizuki.

Great news for the Netherlands was that the other European in the best-16 was compatriot Fleur Smout, and she too made it to the quarterfinal stage. Smout had come through the group stage with good victories against Geraldina Mattson (Great Britain) and Concepcion Garcia (Spain), winning both matches by two *ippon*. Then in the first round she defeated France's Ayana Nakamura, followed by Akiyo Yamaguchi Ellin (NZ) in the second round and Vai Leng Ng of Macao in the third round to set up a quarterfinal with Korea's Y-Y. Hu, who in the third-round had defeated Japan's Tayama. Hu's defeat of Tayama would mean that for only the second time in WKC history, Japan would not occupy the top four spots of the women's individual competition.

At the quarterfinal stage there were three Japanese, two Koreans, two Dutch, and one Canadian.

Matsumoto defeated van der Woude with a *men* and *dō*, but the result probably does not reflect just how close this match was. Japan's Kawagoe Mana fought B-K. Won of Korea. At around the two-minute mark Won took the lead with a strong *kote*. Straight after the restart one flag went up for a *dō* from Kawagoe. Won did not sit back and try to see the match out but went on the attack. That created an opening for Kawagoe and she scored a *men-kaeshi-dō* to even the contest. Another solitary flag went up, this time for a *kote* from Won. After more exchanges, Won sealed it with a *kote*, not long before the end of regulation time. Kawagoe's loss meant that only two Japanese women could finish in the top four.

Smout's great run came to an end when she faced Hu, who in the previous round defeated Tayama. A *men-kaeshi-do* and *kote* sent Hu to the semifinal. The remaining semifinal spot was taken by Takami Yukiko (Japan) after she defeated Canada's Hanaca Yamada with a *men* in *enchō*.

For the first time ever at a WKC, a Korean woman had made it to the semifinal. In fact, there were two: Matsumoto versus Won and Takami versus Hu. In her semifinal, the young Matsumoto had a flag raised for what looked like a solid *men*. At a little under two minutes later, Matsumoto took the lead with a *hiki-men* strike. Matsumoto then booked her place in the final with a men *strike*. On the other court, it was Takami and Hu. About three minutes in, both competitors were given a *hansoku*, most likely for spending too much time in *tsubazeriai*. Close to the end, one dropped *shinai*, stepping out, or more *tsubazeriai* could decide the match. This was a much more cautious match than the other semi with both Takami and Hu not taking any chances. The match headed into *enchō*, and after about fifty seconds, Hu got the *kote* necessary to put the first Korean in a final.

The final got off to a great start with a flurry of exchanges before simmering down. Matsumoto went for *men* and

The Women's Individual Competition Result

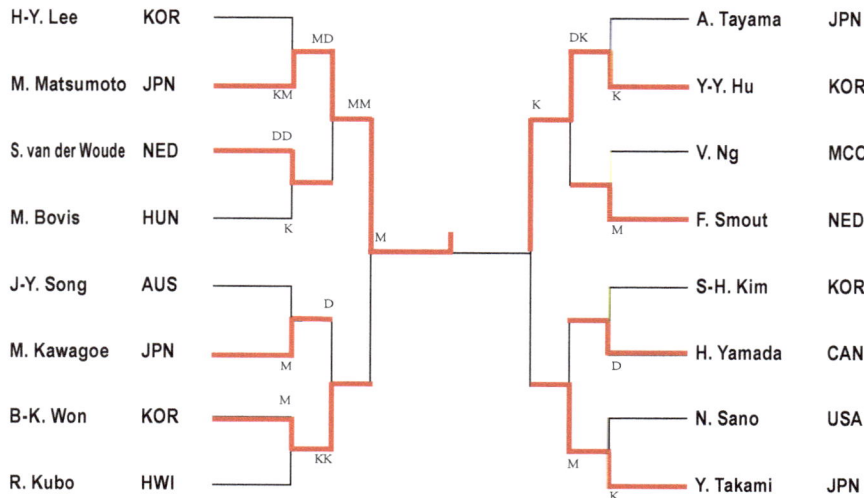

Hu countered with a *kaeshi-dō*. Matsumoto fell heavily in the exchange. The match was stopped and in a great show of sporting goodwill, Hu rushed over to help Matsumoto, which the crowd appreciated. Matsumoto had to take a little time to get herself ready and then the match began again. Hu was given a *hansoku*. The match headed into *enchō*. After a long period of *tsubazeriai*, something that Hu had to be wary of, both competitors moved back to strike *hiki-men* but Matsumoto's was by far the stronger strike and the *ippon* was given.

In recent years there has been much more variation in the top four at the WKC in the men's competition than the women's. The Korean men have been closer to the Japanese, but now with two women in the top four, it certainly looks like the Koreans are catching up to their Japanese counterparts. And let us not forget the European vanguard lead by the Dutch, who had a great showing.

The Women's Team Competition

Not long after the women's individual competition concluded, the women's team event began. Of the five debut nations in this WKC, Indonesia, Mongolia, and Turkey fielded teams. The Indonesians had somewhat of a baptism of fire, being drawn in a group with Hawaii and Korea. Losing 4–0 going into the Taishō match, it looked like it would end 5–0 when Hawaii's Gina Kishimoto scored a *hiki-kote* just over ten seconds into the match. Fiddina Mediola Chaeruddin clearly had not read the script. Kishimoto was not spending much time in *tsubazeriai* in order to eat up time but was instead trying *ōji-waza* to get the point she needed to seal the victory. However, just a matter of seconds before the end, Chaeruddin struck *kote*, Indonesia's second *ippon*, to tie the encounter and finish the match 4–0. Indonesia's final league match was against Korea and they lost 5–0.

Mongolia did not progress but they fared better in the league stage. They lost their first three matches against Ecuador and drew the fourth. Then in the Taishō match,

Mongolia's Zolzaya Sandag scored a *kote* and *kote-nuki-men* in quick succession to give them their only win. Mongolia's other group match was against Thailand. The Mongolian women took the lead in all five matches but in only one could they hang on for the victory and eventually lost 3–1. In the other match in this league, Thailand defeated Ecuador 3–1 to progress to the knock-out stage for the first time in their history.

Turkey was in the only group that had four teams and were with Brazil, Singapore, and Switzerland. This was difficult for them as Singapore was a best-16 team in the last WKC, and Brazil has finished in the top four in all but two of the WKCs to date. Turkey got off to a good start with a 2–1 victory over Switzerland, but then lost 5–0 to Singapore and Brazil, scoring only one *ippon* in the process. Brazil ended up topping this group and Singapore also qualified for the next round by finishing second.

The Japan team, like Korea, was predictably dominant with 5–0 victories over France and Chile without conceding any *ippon* and scoring 18.

Joining Brazil, Japan, Korea, Thailand, and Singapore in the best-16 were Belgium, Canada, Australia, the U.S.A., Italy, the Netherlands, and Finland, who all topped their groups, as well as Chile, Germany, Hawaii and Malaysia, who finished second in their groups.

Moving on to the best-16 round, Japan soundly defeated Belgium 5–0. Belgium have never made it to the quarterfinal stage. Singapore just made it past Thailand in a match that was decided by *ippon* scored after a 2–2 draw. Canada defeated Hawaii 4–0, and the U.S.A made it past Australia 3–1 with the young Kim and Kil getting the U.S.A. off to the perfect start. Brazil, Italy, Germany, and Korea defeated Malaysia, Chile, the Netherlands, and Finland respectively to make it to the quarterfinals.

This was the first time since the women's team competition took its current format at the 11th WKC in 2000 that Australia did not progress to the quarterfinals. Another notable exception was France, who had made it to this stage at every WKC since the 12th WKC in Glasgow.

The quarterfinal round at the 16th WKC was a strong one. Japan and Korea have been ever-present at this stage since the inception of the women's competition, and Brazil, Canada, and the U.S.A. have each missed out on only one occasion. This was Germany's fourth consecutive appearance at this stage and Italy's first since 2003. Only Singapore had never made it to this stage; in fact, this was actually Singapore's first time to qualify from the league.

It was unfortunate for Singapore then, that they had to meet Japan in the quarterfinal. They were beaten 5–0, losing each match by two *ippon*, but overall they should be pleased with their performance as they made it a lot

further than they ever had before.

In the Canada/U.S.A. quarterfinal, again it was Kim and Kil who got the U.S.A. off to a great start. The Chūken match between Canada's Bree Yang and the U.S.A.'s Nishiki Sano ended in a draw and then Hanaca Yamada pulled one back for Canada after initially going one point down against Sumi Domen. Akiko Fukushima needed to beat Kaori Kikunaga by two *ippon* to keep Canada in it and force a *daihyō-sen*. It was not to be, however, as Taishō Kikunaga scored a great *men* and a solid *kote* to finish the match and send the U.S.A. into their fourth semifinal in six attempts.

Brazil defeated Italy 4–0 to put them in their third consecutive semifinal, and Germany were defeated 5–0 by Korea. The teams making up the semifinal were the same as those at the 15th WKC with the exception of the U.S.A. taking the place of Germany. The first semifinal was between Japan and the U.S.A. The last time they met was in the semifinal of the 14th WKC. In that match Japan won 5–0, and that was the result this time.

In the next semifinal, Brazil faced Korea. Their most recent meeting was at the same stage of the 15th WKC, and Korea won that encounter 3–0. At the 16th WKC, S-A. Jung gave Korea a 1–0 lead with a single *men* strike in a close match with Aline Kimura. Y-Y. Hu strengthened Korea's grip on the semifinal by defeating Cristiane Toida with two *men* strikes, the first of which came very soon after Toida was given a *hansoku* for stepping out of bounds. In the Chūken match, Korea's B-K. Won took a men *ippon*. If the match ended like this, Brazil were out. Won was just too strong for Marcia Hayashi as she took another *men* to send Korea to the final.

Playing for pride, Brazil's Eliete Takashina faced H-Y. Lee. Things started badly for Takashina as she conceded a *men* from Lee's first attack. Takashina went on the offensive and had a good shout for *men*, but nothing was given. Takashina's perseverance paid off. Lee was pressuring Takashina and the latter was moving back slightly. Lee thought she had the opening for *kote* and committed, but Takashina scored a great *kote-nuki-men* to tie the match. After a few more exchanges, again Lee went for *kote* and again Takashina executed what looked a good *kote-nuki-men* which got one flag raised. The match was decided when Lee made yet another attempt at *kote*, but this time got it spot on and it scored.

Korea were now leading 4–0 moving into the Taishō match between Brazil's Miwa Onaka and Korea's S-H. Kim. Onaka appeared in the 10th WKC back in 1997 and was the runner-up in the women's individual under 2-dan competition. She has been a fixture in the Brazil team since then. About one minute in, Onaka moved forward and raised her shinai as if going to strike *men*. Kim reacted but Onaka turned her wrists and struck *kote*. There was no doubt and all three *shinpan* raised their

flags. The match restarted and after several exchanges, Kim equalised when Onaka attempted *men* which was countered with *kaeshi-dō*. The match did not stay like this for long as, in the same way as her first *ippon*, Onaka moved for *men* but changed to *kote* and scored to finish the semifinal 4–1.

So, for the fourth consecutive WKC, the final would be Japan versus Korea. First up was Sakuma Yoko and S-A. Jung. This match got off to an electric start with an *ippon* almost scored within three seconds! Right from the outset Sakuma moved forward and went for *men*. Jung moved back slightly to avoid the strike but Sakuma kept going forward and both struck *men* simultaneously. Both looked in. One flag went up for Sakuma; one for Kim. The *shushin* looked in two minds and half raised one and then the other before disagreeing with both. At that moment, Miyazaki Masahiro-sensei, the Japan team manager raised his own flag to query the decision. A *gōgi* was called which resulted in no *ippon* being awarded. The slow motion replay does show that Sakuma's *men* landed first, but even in slow motion it was hard to tell. The match continued. Both competitors had a few good calls. After a short period in *tsubazeriai*, both Sakuma and Kim tried *hiki-men*, but it was Sakuma's that landed a fraction of a second earlier to get the *ippon*, which was enough to win.

The Jihō match was between Takahashi Moeko and Y-Y. Hu. Takahashi had the first good attempt, a *men*, but Hu was using her physicality and height advantage to keep pushing Takahashi away from her to open up a good *maai* to be able to strike. As Takahashi was coaxed into making a *men* strike, Hu countered and scored with a *men-kaeshi-do*, but as she went through her trailing leg caught Takahashi's and she fell awkwardly on her left elbow. A long break followed while she got treatment.

The Women's Team Competition Result

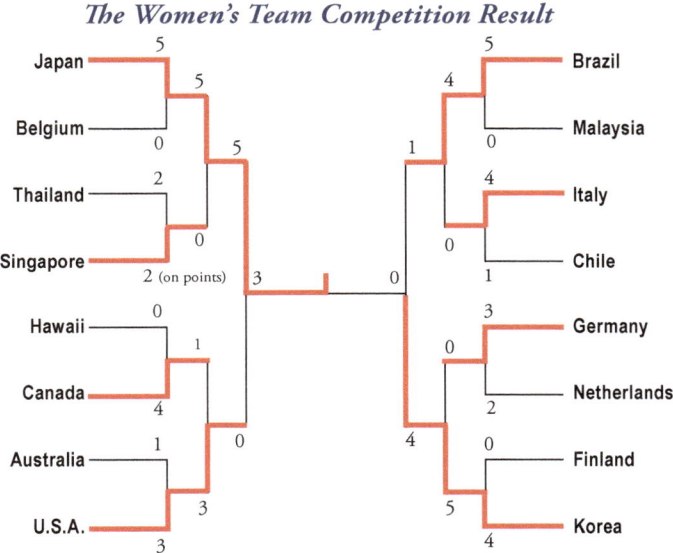

Hu was not separating and subsequently given a *hansoku*. Immediately after the restart Takahashi rushed forwards with her *shinai* slightly raised. Hu went for *men* but that was countered with a fantastic *dō* strike. Hu did not look happy with herself. The aggression from both competitors got ratcheted up after the restart, so much so that Takahashi was given a *hansoku*. The match ended 1–1, and Japan had conceded their first *ippon* of the 16th WKC.

The Chūken match between Watanabe Tai and M-J. Cha ended in a *hikiwake* with no *ippon* scored. It was not through lack of trying though as this was a great match with lots of chances from both competitors. The energy from the previous three matches found its way into this encounter between Yamamoto Mariko and B-K. Won. Both Yamamoto and Won had periods where they were being the more aggressive and pressuring their opponent more. It was a rip-roaring match. The only *ippon* of the match finally came, a *de-gote* from Yamamoto, about 45 seconds from the end. Instead of sitting on that *ippon*, Yamamoto was still looking for the winning point. Won made several attempts but could not get anything and the match finished 1–0 which gave the championship to Japan.

Matsumoto Mizuki met S-H. Kim in the Taishō match, the result of which would now be academic. Matsumoto scored with her first strike, a *kote*.

Even though Korea lost 3–0, the match was closer than the result suggests. This has to have been the best women's team final held so far and it showed a level of physicality and aggression that had not been seen before. Japan and Korea are still a distance ahead of the U.S.A. and Brazil, but, as this WKC showed, the gap is getting closer.

In its current format the women's individual and team events are held on the same day and all matches are four minutes in duration, unlike the men's five minutes. Talking to the female competitors, there have been calls to make the women's matches five minutes in duration, too. If this happens, then surely, like the men's events, the women's individual and team events must be held over two days. It will be interesting to see if any changes will be made for the 17th WKC in Korea.

The Men's Team Competition

As noted above, the men's team event drew the biggest crowd of the three days. This was also the only day that had live coverage on NHK, Japan's national broadcaster.

Of the 16 groups in the league stage, four of them

contained four teams and they all had one of the top-four teams from the WKC in 2012: Japan, Korea, the U.S.A., and Hungary. As was to be expected, Japan and Korea were dominant throughout. In the league stage, Japan faced Canada, Sweden and Norway. Japan's first match was against Canada. Expecting a tough test from Canada, Japan fielded a strong team with Takenouchi Yūya, Katsumi Yōsuke, Shōdai Masahirō, Andō Shō and Uchimura Ryōichi. This team proved to be too strong for Canada as they were brushed aside 5–0.

In their next match, Takenouchi and Uchimura were rested and in came Masuda Ryō and Yamada Ryōhei, who was a high school student when selected for the Japan team. In the Senpō match, Masuda took the lead with a *dō* against Goran Guitierrez-Aranda, who equalised with a *kote*. That would be one of only three *ippon* that Japan conceded until the final. Yamada beat Ren Watanabe with a solitary *men* strike and the remaining three matches were all won by two *ippon*. In their final league match, Japan beat Norway 5–0 without conceding a point and scoring two *ippon* in each match. In the other matches in that league, Sweden beat Norway 4–1 and Canada beat Sweden 3–0 and Norway 4–0. Qualifying from a group with either Japan or Korea is always going to be a tough task…

Korea were also in a four-team league. First they faced WKC debutantes Turkey and won 4–0 with Senpō J-Y. Jo unable to score against Cihan Engin. Korean Taishō K-H. Lee, who has been a fixture in the Korean team for years, beat Can Aydogdu with *kote* but could not get the second *ippon*. Then Korea faced Italy, who certainly did not make things easy for them. Korea won 3–0 without conceding a point. In their final league match they brushed aside Finland 5–0 scoring two *ippon* in each match.

Hungary, who finished third in the previous WKC made it from their group with Australia, Chile, and Romania. They beat Romania 5–0, Australia 5–0, and Chile 3–2, with both Attila and Sandor Dubi losing to Tomas Miranda, a former International Budo University student and Kendo World team member, and Stefan Domancic respectively. Romania lost all of their matches (2–0 against Chile, and 4–0 to Australia).

The other four-team league featured the U.S.A, France, Greece and Malaysia. First, the U.S.A. fought France with Danny Yang as Senpō and Chris Yang as Taishō getting their only wins. Next the U.S.A. faced Malaysia and beat them 5–0 and finished their matches with a 4–0 victory over Greece.

None of the debut federations progressed to the tournament stage. Croatia lost to both Great Britain and New Zealand; Indonesia to Thailand and the Netherlands; Mongolia to China and Montenegro; and Turkey to Korea, Finland, and Italy. Still, this was their first step onto the world stage and will no doubt be a valuable learning experience.

Ireland made their WKC debut in 2003 in Glasgow, and they had never made it past the league stage before, but that changed at the N*ippon* Budokan. Their first match against South Africa was very close. It was tied at 1-1 going into the Taishō match but South Africa were ahead on *ippon*. In order to make sure that Ireland definitively won that match, Lee Cahill had to score two *ippon* without conceding one, which he duly did. Ireland then booked their place in the knockout stages with a 3–1 victory over Latvia. However, Ireland's good run would come to end as they met Korea and were defeated 5–0.

China made their debut in the 14th WKC in Brazil and got as far as the best-16. In only their third WKC they again made it to the best-16 stage with 5–0 and 4–0 wins over Mongolia and Montenegro respectively. In the best 16 round at the N*ippon* Budokan they met Spain, who had a convincing win over Switzerland and a close match with Russia in the league stage. The Spanish Senpō, Lucas Pina, gave Spain an early lead with a solid *kote* strike, but the Chinese *nitō* kendoka Lunwei Zhang won the Jihō match and the Chinese Chūken Zhonglin Zhang won to take the score to 2–1. Xuan Chen took the lead against Markel Arregui but conceded two *ippon* to lose the fourth match. The Spanish Taishō then had to win the match; a draw would not suffice due to China's superior number of *ippon* scored. Guillermo Serra knew what he had to do against Ganfeng Yang and got off to good start with a great *kote*. However, not long before the end, Yang equalised with a *hiki-men*.

If the result stayed the same, Spain would not go through. However, with Yang's *ippon*, Serra had no choice but to go for it. Twice Yang bundled Serra out of the court; the second time resulted in a *hansoku*. Almost straight after that *hansoku*, Yang stuck himself to Serra so that the latter could not attack, knowing that if the match stayed as it was, China would progress. Yang was subsequently given a *hansoku* of his own. Soon after, the match ended and China progressed to the quarterfinal in only their third WKC.

The 16th WKC

Hungary met Belgium in the best-16 round and got off to a bad start, losing the first two matches 2–1 to Kensaku Maemoto and Peter D'Hont. However, last year's best-4 finishers showed their resolve and Gabor Babos, Attila Dubi and Sandor Dubi each won their matches 2–0 to send Hungary to the quarterfinal for the third consecutive WKC.

In the first of the quarterfinal matches, Japan beat Brazil 5–0 but Jihō Katsumi got off to a troubled start after conceding a *dō* strike to Alberto Takayama. Hungary met China and progressed to the semifinal for the second consecutive WKC by winning 3–1, and the U.S.A. defeated Chinese Taipei 4–1. The remaining quarterfinal match was Korea and Mexico.

Korea's great form continued as they beat Mexico 5–0, scoring ten points and conceding only one. In the Jihō match, Korea's giant M-U. Jang scored a terrific *men*, but Guillermo Flores lured Jang into going for *men* and struck *degote*, which the crowd at the Nippon Budokan loved. Jang could not score the point he needed and started to attack relentlessly, appearing to get frustrated as he was roughhousing Flores. The *shinpan* called a *gōgi* but no *hansoku* was given. Flores' brave stand ended when Jang finished the match with a *men*. Korea then won the rest of the matches to set up a quarterfinal with the U.S.A.

Mexico had a great WKC, as reaching the quarterfinals was their best performance to date. They went one better than the previous tournament in Italy when they progressed to the best-16 for the second time, but were comprehensively beaten by NZ 5–0 then. The first time they reached the best-8 was at the 8th WKC in Toronto, 1991.

The semifinal round turned out to be a carbon copy of the 15th WKC: Japan/Hungary and the U.S.A./Korea. Japan were just too good for Hungary and won 5–0, but Chūken Gabor Babos did take the first *ippon*, a *kote*, against Shodai. This was the same score as in the 15th WKC. The U.S.A. and Korea semifinal was a much closer match. Korean Senpō J-Y. Jo put Korea in the lead with two men *ippon* against Sandip Ghogaonkar. The next three matches were all draws with only the Fukushō match seeing any *ippon* scored. B-H. Park scored a solid *tsuki* against Brandon Harada. If the match ended like this, it would have sent Korea to the final. Harada, however, had other ideas. Harada started to attack *men*, and had a couple of good attempts, and *kote*, too. Just a matter of seconds before the end, Harada was retreating and Park followed. Harada stopped and immediately started to move forward while raising the tip of his *shinai*. Park started to raise his and Harada took what has to be one of the best *kote* strikes from this WKC. That meant that in the Taisho match Chris Yang would have to win 2–0 to force the *daihyō-sen* playoff. It was not to be, however. From *tsubazeriai*, Lee scored *hiki-dō* and finished the match with a *kote* to send Korea to the final with a 2–0 victory. The matches between Korea and the U.S.A. have been very close for the last few WKC. Korea won 2–0 in the final at the 13th WKC, and 3–2 in the 15th WKC semifinal so the U.S.A. is definitely closing the gap.

For the second consecutive WKC, and ninth time overall, Korea would face Japan in the final, and it was not without moments of controversy. In the Senpō match, Takenouchi faced M-U. Jang. Both Takenouchi and Jang had some good attempts at men, and Takenouchi had a particularly good attempt at *kote*. About 45 seconds before the end, Lee moved in and raised his *shinai*. Takenouchi also raised his but with the *kensen* pointing to his right and angled slightly down as if trying to protect his *kote*. Jang lowered his *shinai*, turned his wrists, and struck what looked like a great, solid *kote*. Takenouchi countered and struck a *men* that barely looked in. All the flags went up for Takenouchi's *men* at which Jang looked surprised. Some people have said that Jang's *kote* was more of a slap than a strike, but no matter how many times we see that *ippon* on video, it is clearly Jang's *kote*. It happened so quickly that it is easy to see how a mistake could have been made.

The Jihō match was between Katsumi and J-Y. Jo who took two great *men* in quick succession to put Korea even. In the Chūken match, B-H. Park struck what looked like a great *hiki-men* against Shōdai. Most of the crowd thought it was in, and the replays seem to suggest that, but the *shinpan* did not think so. Shortly after, Shōdai pressured Park and as he raised his *shinai*, Shodai struck *kote*. This one is debatable, too, as replays show that Shōdai actually struck Park's left hand near the *tsuka-gashira*. There was no mistake with Shōdai's second *kote*, which was scored immediately after the restart.

With Japan leading 2–1, Andō faced J-M. Yu in the Fukushō match. The match started aggressively, but that aggression soon died down with strikes coming few and far between. Both competitors were being cautious with Yu knowing that if he lost, the title was Japan's, and Andō knowing that if he lost, it would come down to the Taishō. They were spending a lot of time in *tsubazeriai* with Andō appearing not to separate. Twice the *shinpan* called "*wakare*", but they went back into *tsubazeriai*.

Korea

USA
5
USA

USA
USA
1

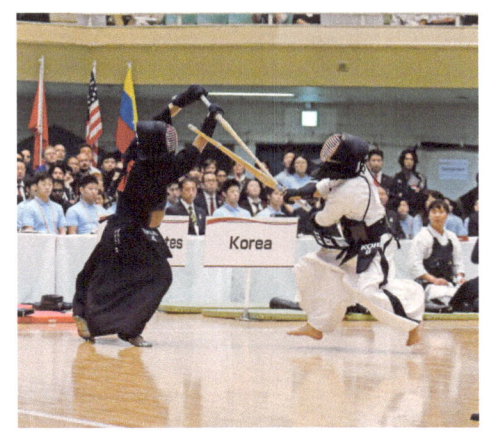

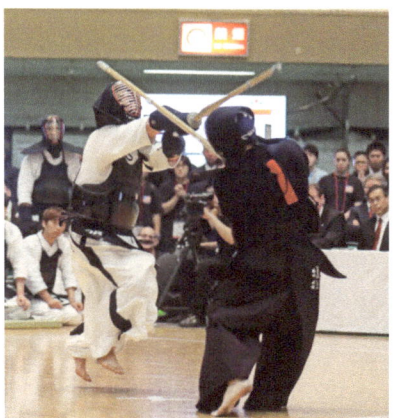

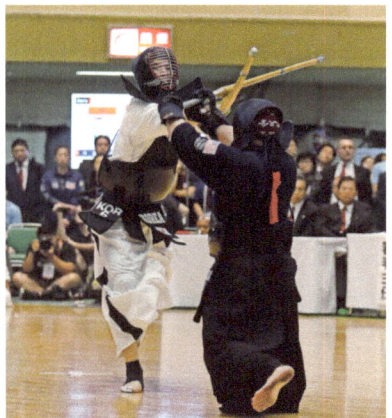

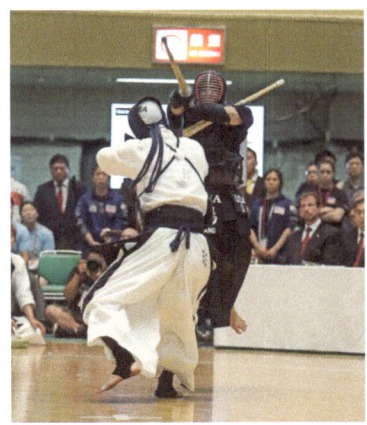

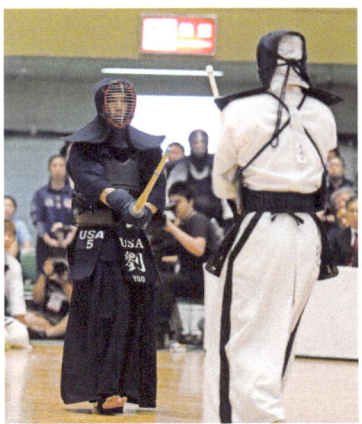

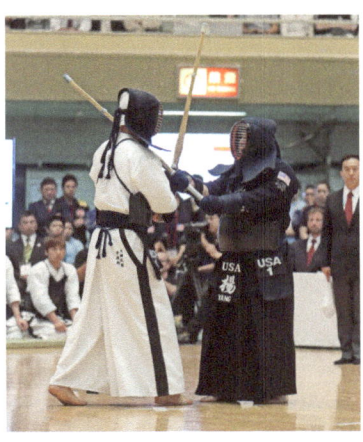

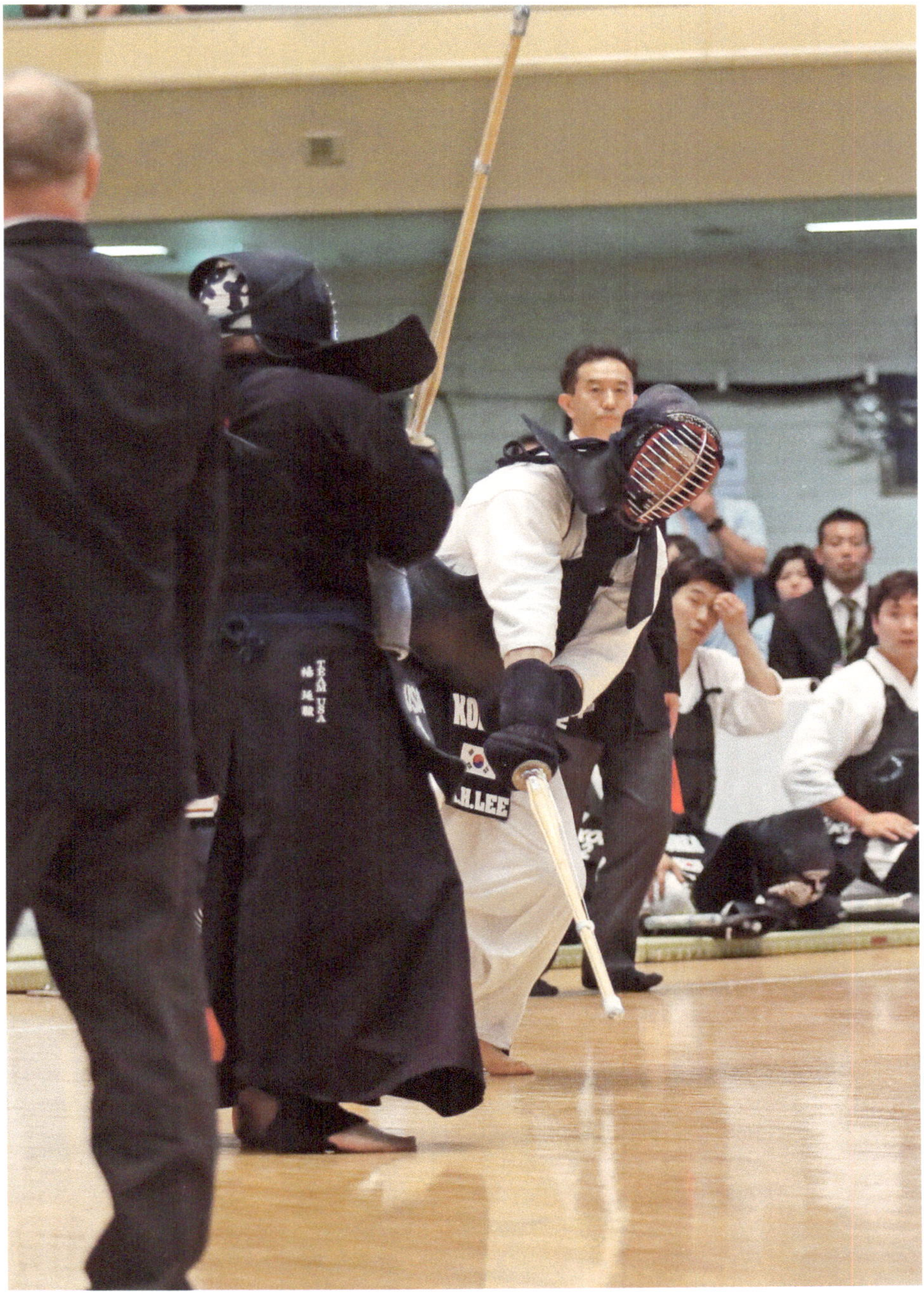
TEAM USA

It looked like Andō was deliberately placing his *shinai* on Yu's left shoulder so that he was unable to make a strike. The *shinpan* called a halt to the match and after a *gōgi*, Ando was given a *hansoku*. After a short burst of striking, Ando's *shinai* went back again and again onto Yu's shoulder and the crowd groaned as this continued to happen. Again a *gōgi* was called, but no second *hansoku* was given to Andō; even he looked surprised. The match ended in a draw, but should Lee have won by a hansoku? We heard one comment that Andō was being very cynical in knowing that, considering the arena and the stage, he would not be given a second *hansoku*. Whether that is actually the case or not is up for debate, but if the *shushin* called a *gōgi*, it is probably because he thought that it warranted a further penalty.

In the Taishō match, Uchimura had to at least draw with K-H. Lee to make Japan champions. It would not have been surprising to have seen Uchimura shut up shop, and while at times he did rush in to *tsubazeriai* to prevent Lee from striking, he made several attacks. Lee was the more aggressive and on many occasions was pushing Uchimura back to try and create some space so that he could attack. In the end, Uchimura was able to hold on for the draw and Japan were able to take their fifteenth title.

It was a great three days at the Nippon Budokan where kendo "came home". Kendo World had many people visit our shop to buy some books and magazines, or just pop by for a chat at our stall.

Don't forget that we produced a 16th WKC Special Issue that is on sale now in POD and Zinio formats. Search for "Kendo World – Special Edition".

Well, there's only three years to wait until the next WKC in Korea. We hope to see you there!

The Men's Team Competition Result

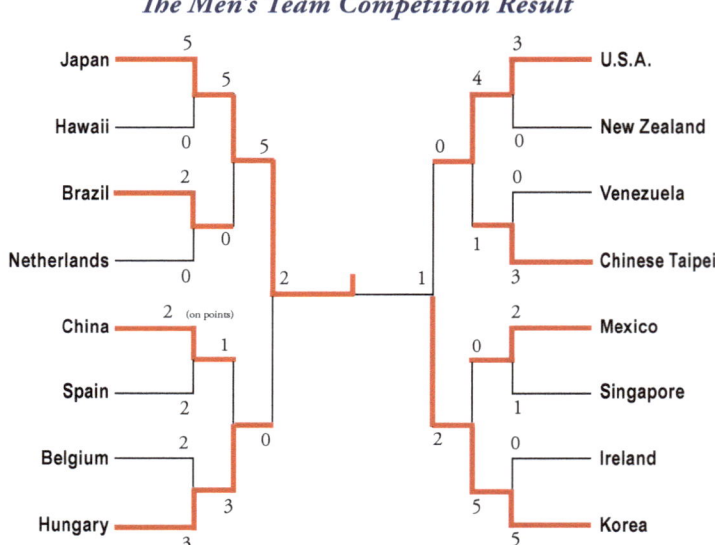

The 16th WKC

Reflections on the Women's Competition at the 16th World Kendo Championships

By Kate Sylvester

The 16th World Kendo Championships held at the Nippon Budokan May 29-31, 2015, were the first time that women have competed in Japan as official WKC competitors. At the 10th WKC in Kyoto in 1997, the last time it was held in Japan, the women's competition was unofficial. The Nippon Budokan is considered to be the budo mecca where the most famous *shiaisha* in Japan have competed for decades. Saturday May 30, was a day of truth and opportunity for the assembled female competitors. Spectators filled the Budokan's tiers in the greatest number of people that they would probably ever compete in front of. Luck would be on the side of those who had given their all in preparation, and those who could manage the pressure of expectation and the magnificence of the venue.

At every WKC there is increased participation by women. The 16th WKC was comprised of 154 competitors in the women's individual event, and 34 women's teams. This is a marked increase from the 15th WKC where there were only 132 individual competitors and 30 teams. Some women's teams who have attended past WKCs, such as New Zealand and Hungary, disappointingly did not compete in the team event, but many new ones were present.

From the beginning of the day of women's competition there was a noticeable improvement in the level of international women's kendo. Impressively, European kendo is producing some skilled female kendoka such as Alina Gdeczyk (Poland), Asteria Akila (Greece), Serena

Ricciuti (Italy), Pauline Stolarz (France), Safiyah Fadai (Germany) and Sayo van der Woude (Netherlands), to name but a few. Despite this increase in level, Japan and Korea proved to be indomitable as they outclassed their opponents and took the top four places in the individual event. In the history of the WKC, only once has Japan failed to take all top four places in the women's individual event. That was at the 14th WKC held in Brazil in 2009, where E. Takashina (Brazil) took bronze. However, this year Korea proved a greater challenge to Japan's domination by taking two of the top-4 places.

For the first time in history it was a Japan-Korea final in the women's individual competition between Mizuki Matsumoto (Japan) and Yun Yung Hu (Korea). The reign of Japanese women's kendo lay on the shoulders of 22-year-old Kanagawa policewoman, Matsumoto Mizuki. In *enchō*, Matsumoto struck a clean *hiki-men* against Hu to win the individual title. Matsumoto's win was the starting point for the Japanese women's team to continue a strong performance throughout the team competition.

This was a WKC where anything could happen. Many teams had new and inexperienced players that could work either for or against them. There were some upsets, such as France losing to Chile early on in the pools. The U.S.A. had two outstanding players: 17-year-old Esther Kim and Yuri Kil (16), who knocked out their opponents with convincing wins. This helped the U.S.A. to finish third—their best result since 2009. Brazil, constant favourites led by the experienced Miwa Onaka, once again finished in third place also.

In spite of the skill of fresh international players, Japan and Korea are still considerably ahead. However, it seems that the gap between Japan and Korea has become smaller. Japan averaged 5 match wins in all their team matches while Korea averaged 4 match wins. The Japan-Korea final promised an action-packed finish to the day.

There was something outstanding about the Japanese women's team at this WKC. The Japanese women had strategy and physical power which set them above the other nations. In the final, Miyazaki-sensei strategically changed the team order, placing the team captain, Yoko Sakuma as Senpō, and one of the youngest players, Matsumoto Mizuki, as Taishō. Throughout all the matches, the Japanese women's team fought with confidence, skill and power, which was in direct contrast to the 2012 WKC where the Japanese women fought with defensive

kendo. It seemed as though there was little Korea could do to gain a lead after a strong start from Sakuma with her *men* and unshakeable confidence inspiring the rest of her team. Matsumoto once again sealed victory for Japan by winning her match with *kote* as Taishō.

Although the level of international women's kendo is improving, Japan's level is seemingly becoming unreachable. This may be due to the high level of coaching they received from Miyazaki-sensei, and the fact that he has coached the women's team for a second consecutive campaign. There has also been a gradual increase in the prestige of women's kendo in Japan with more high level competitions and *tokuren* (elite kendo squad) positions in the nation's police force.

Often when the prestige of women in hegemonic masculine sports is increased, the presence of male coaches and administrators in such women's sports also increases disproportionately. Miyazaki-sensei surprised many when he collected the women's team championship prize in 2012 in Italy. Once again at the Nippon Budokan, he collected the first-place prize and the Korean coach followed by collecting the second-place prize. In the men's team competition, the male captains collected the prizes, not the coaches. What do future WKCs hold for women's kendo? An increase or decrease in marginalization and inequality of women in kendo? Let us see in Korea 2018.

Kendo Wa:
A Film Series About World Kendo

Canadian kenshi and filmmaker documents Team Canada and the 16th WKC to tell stories of international kendo

By Charlie Kondek

"To have Team Canada face off against Team Japan in the World Champs at the Budokan? I couldn't have scripted it any better."

These are Simon Conlin's words. *Kendo Wa* is not his film. At least, not his alone. Rather, it is a collaboration between Conlin and many other people, including the Canadian national kendo team that competed at the 16th World Kendo Championships in Tokyo this year, and, if all goes according to Conlin's strategy, the global kendo community.

With this epic match as its centrepiece, *Kendo Wa* will tell the stories of kendo's rich 100+ year history in Canada, the legacy of Team Canada's previous participation in the WKC, and the individual stories of the people involved, whether as team members, coaches, fellow trainees or supporters.

There's no denying Conlin is a driving force behind the film aiming for an October, 2015 release. When complete, *Kendo Wa* will be a documentary about Team Canada's training and participation in the 16th WKC.

The film takes its name from a concept that means, among other things, "team harmony". Some feel it is a fundamental concept not just for kendo but of Japanese society in general. Conlin envisions a film about 42 minutes in length, broken into about eight episodes, all available online. And, it is online that more of *Kendo Wa*'s collaborators, the global kendo community, have played a lead role. So far, the film has successfully raised over $8,000 to help towards production costs through online crowdfunding. Approximately $8,000 in the form of in-kind sponsorships from companies such as Panasonic Canada has also been secured, helping the film reach its

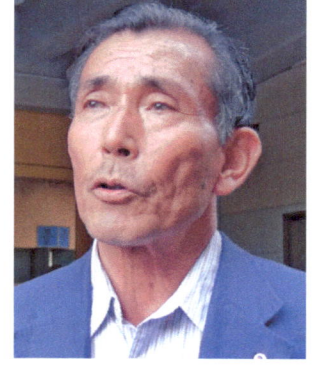

modest budget of $16,000. But *Kendo Wa* will also rely on the digital reach of the world kendo community for distribution via sharing in social media.

According to Conlin's vision, *Kendo Wa* is not just the story of Canadian kendo. With the 16th WKC as its stage, it is a story of international kendo and the strength and spirit of all the nations that compete there. One could argue that, ultimately, the team focused on in the "team harmony" theme of the film is not just Canada, but the entire kendo community. To an extent, Conlin and the filmmakers are telling everyone's story.

The project is a natural for choice as Conlin has worked as a digital content creator and strategist in marketing for over 15 years. A 4-dan in kendo and *ikkyū* in both iaido and jodo at Toronto Kendo Club, Conlin, originally from the UK, has practised kendo since he was a young boy. Several trends converged to inspire Conlin to make the film. He says that, thanks to the internet and online video, there's been an increasing volume of kendo content available. The tools for filmmaking have also gotten better. Early in his career, Conlin was interested in online visual and audio content. He was approached by Adobe in late 2013 to make an online promotional video using its new suite of Premier editing tools, and a collection of state-of-the-art cameras. Naturally, his preferred subject was kendo. Parts of the footage he made for Adobe, which went on to be shown at some of the world's largest film industry events and trade shows, such as SIGGRAPH 2014 and NAB 2014, can be seen in the trailer for *Kendo Wa*.

Conlin was hungry to see what else he could do. "I've got the bug for it now," he remembers thinking. "It's such a nice

way to promote kendo and to inspire younger generations." The 16th WKC was the perfect moment in time, providing the setting, plot and characters for the documentary film. "It's just an epic story," Conlin said.

When he approached Team Canada with the concept for *Kendo Wa*, Bryan Asa, R6-dan, of the Japanese Canadian Cultural Centre club in Toronto, and Shigemitsu Kamata, 6-dan, of the nearby Etobicoke Kendo Olympium Kendo/Iaido Club were very receptive, and have helped mentor the project ever since. Both R6-dan Hyun-Jun Choi (VP East of the CKF) of Jung-ko Kendo Club and K7-dan Alex Bennett of Kendo World have also been very inspirational and an integral part of this project. On the film's lean crew are Patrick Barfoot, editor, Rob Butterwick, cameraman, Kevin Ip, camera and editing, and Alfred Lanin, a media student of Seneca College of Applied Arts and Technology in Canada.

The technique of the filmmakers is to capture footage when they can (limited by opportunity and budget) of Team Canada training and discussing their motivations, methods, challenges, and hopes. Conlin and Ip accompanied Team Canada to Tokyo for the 16th WKC, and were on hand to capture all the action on (and off) the *shiai-jō*, as well as interviews with other kenshi from around the world.

Next comes editing. Conlin and crew have to go through hours of video to get the right few minutes for the final cut. But they also have to discern the stories and cull them into a narrative. "There's post-it notes on a board everywhere," Conlin explained. "How does this story connect to this story?" The crew has plenty of action footage and also exclusive interviews from sensei and kenshi such as H8-dan Sumi Masatake (JPN), K8-dan Ozawa Hiroshi (JPN), H8-dan Morito Tsumura (CAN), K8-dan Shigetaka "Shane" Kamata (CAN), K7-dan Taro Ariga (USA), K7-dan Alex Bennett (NZ), and R7-dan Kiwada Daisuke (JPN). Also interviewed were K7-dan Shigeo Kimura-sensei (CAN) and K7-dan Geoff Salmon (GB), both of whom were *shinpan* at the 16th WKC.

Although not new to film media, this is Conlin's first documentary. Still, his previous experience gives him confidence. "When you've worked long enough in digital and social media you constantly have to re-learn the rules, and adapt all the time." The method so far has been to let the story flow naturally and evolve.

There's a lot to tell. Kendo has existed in Canada since the early 1900s, and its practitioners see themselves as inheritors of a legacy that is uniquely Canadian as well as Japanese, national, societal and personal. *Kendo Wa* tells the story of this diverse legacy as it meets with the traditions of kendo in other nations—including Japan, the powerful team that Canada had to face in the preliminary heats in the men's division.

By now you know the results, but *Kendo Wa* will tell the story in ways you can't experience anywhere else. With strong players—men and women—how will this story unfold in the external action of swordplay and on the internal human hearts of the kendoka and supporters? We can look forward to finding out. We can all pitch in by helping distribute it across the world via social media.

Be sure to visit the following websites:
www.kendowa.com
Facebook.com/KendoWa

KENDO FOR ADULTS

By Hatano Toshio (Courtesy of Kendo Nihon)
Translated by Alex Bennett

Hatano Toshio-sensei was born in January 1945 in Musashi Murayama, Tokyo. After graduating from Kokushikan High School and Nihon University, he became a salaryman for a few years before establishing the Nanbudō Kendōgu shop in 1971. He passed the 8-dan exam on his second attempt in 1994. He serves as an advisor for the West Tokyo Kendo Federation, and is Suruga University Kendo Club Shihan, Musashi Murayama City Kendo Federation President, and leader of the Kinryūkan Dojo.

Part 2: Correct Grip Forms the Basis of Basics

There is a tenet of wisdom from the Yagyū Shinkage-ryū: "Break away from the teachings, but remember the teachings…" The *Analects of Confucius* state: "At 15, I had my mind set on learning. At 30, I stood firm. At 40, I had no doubts. At 50, I knew the decrees of Heaven. At 60, my ear was an obedient organ for the reception of truth. At 70, I could follow what my heart desired, without transgressing what was right." These two teachings are essentially the same thing. The *Analects* are much older than the Yagyū school of swordsmanship, so it stands to reason that Yagyū Sekishūsai Muneyoshi was referring to Confucius.

Thinking about Confucius's admission that he started studying at the age of 15 and finally reached an understanding of the ultimate truth when he was 70 reminds me of the great kendo master, Mochida Moriji 10-dan Hanshi. "It took me 50 years to master the basics of kendo…" This famous quote by Mochida-sensei has flummoxed many high-ranking kenshi. "If it took Mochida-sensei 50 years, how on earth are we supposed to master the basics?!" I think this is missing his point. "Break away from the teachings, but remember the teachings" means that you can do the basics without having to think about them.

Regardless of how high his grade was, did Mochida-sensei always practise *kirikaeshi* and the basics? I don't think that he did. I think that each day he trained, he thought about things such as how to hold the *shinai* properly, and the best way to move. Even with each *men* strike, he surely assessed himself as if he was an examiner on a grading panel. So, after 50 years, he was able to execute all of his strikes without the need to think about them. This is what I believe he meant by his now famous comment.

I often see 7-dan kenshi who are trying for the 8-dan examination ask to do *kihon* after finishing *jigeiko*. They request to do *kirikaeshi* and basic *men* strikes, but I have my misgivings about this. Why don't they strike *men* correctly when they are engaged in *jigeiko*? I imagine it is because during *jigeiko*, they only want to hit their opponent without getting struck themselves. Therefore, in the case of a *men* strike, for example, they attempt to execute the technique in a way that connects with the opponent, but is not in line with proper *kihon*.

"If I strike *men* the *kihon* way, my opponent will hit my *kote*, or counter me easily with some other technique…" Such a sentiment shows that the build-up before striking *men* is inadequate. In other words, there is no psychological pressure being applied—no clash of the minds. The kenshi only desires to hit the target. Those who are aspiring to pass high grades must be aware of this pitfall.

People in the real world who have work and family obligations are lucky to train once or twice a week. Most members in my dojo fall into this category. As soon as they put their *men* on, they jump straight into *jigeiko*. They hardly ever engage in basic training like they did as kids. I think this is fairly standard in most community dojo, and is why it is imperative to think about correct *kihon* while doing *jigeiko*.

Your Grip Shows in Your Kote

The basis for correct *kihon* lies in how you hold the *shinai*. In other words, your grip. Many people overlook this important point. I am often left disappointed when I see how people hold their *bokutō* in kata examinations. They are most likely holding the *bokutō* in the same mistaken way as they grip the *shinai*, only it is less obvious because of the *kote*. This can be said of people of all *dan* ranks; If only they learned to fix their grip, their strikes would be so much stronger.

How should one hold the *shinai*? First, the right hand. I frequently come across people with their right thumb placed loosely on top of the *shinai* hilt. Furthermore, the remaining four fingers are splayed open. This is evident by the shape of their *kote*: the top of the kote fist will be out of shape. People who hold their *shinai* in this way generally seek to make fast, light taps to the target.

They will be unable to make the strong, decisive strikes born of a firm grip. If their opponent is coming forward, they may be able to get a little bit more power in the attack; but if they initiate the strike it will be weak, and probably won't even reach. The *kensen* will be ineffectual, and they will be incapable of making big strikes. Considering that the original meaning of "strike" in kendo is to "cut", it stands to reason that big swings are necessary. Strong swings result in decisive strikes with "*sae*", or crispness. Kenshi who do not employ adequate power in their swings might seem fast in their younger years and will be able to compensate for a time, but will peter out as they get older. It is better to recognise this flaw early on, and fix one's grip to enable bigger, stronger strikes.

When holding the *shinai* in the ready position, the forefinger through to the little finger grip the *shinai* from underneath, and the thumb is wrapped over the top. If the thumb is placed on the very top of the hilt, this indicates that there is no balance in the grip, and the *shinai* will wobble as a result. To prevent this, the joint of the thumb should be squeezed inwards, and the thumbnail should be directed to a spot 1–1.5m in front of the body.

The way the *shinai* is gripped with each finger is slightly different. With the left hand, consciousness (not strength) of the little finger should be at 100%, the ring finger at 90%, middle finger at 80%, and forefinger at 70%. On the right hand, consciousness of the little finger is 80%, ring finger 70%, middle finger 60%, and the forefinger is 50%. Consciousness of the thumb should be 100% for either hand.

Hatano-sensei's kote are on the left. The kote on the right reveal that the right thumb is positioned incorrectly in kamae.

Make sure that there are no gaps between the fingers and thumb; they should be lightly touching. This way, it is easy to tighten the grip enough on impact. If there are gaps between the fingers, it will be impossible to squeeze the hand properly to enact a decisive strike, and generate speed in the cut.

One of my favourite authors once wrote that "Trying to do something that is wrong from the outset is like attempting to force an elephant through the eye of a needle." Mastering something requires considerable repetition and hard work. But, it must be done correctly, otherwise you will master something that is wrong, and hence difficult to fix later. If you train the wrong way, you might as well try and force an elephant through a tiny hole, especially if you are attempting to acquire higher grades.

*Matsudaira Mikiyo's Experience

"For the longest time, I always placed my thumb on the top of the *shinai*. I was good at striking small *men* (*sashi-men*) which is why I held my *shinai* like this. But I often felt that my strikes were only grazing the target. Now that my thumb and fingers hold the *shinai* differently, I feel that my overall striking has improved greatly."

Matsudaira Mikiyo started kendo as a primary school student. She belonged to the Chiba University Kendo Club, and continued after gaining employment at an airline company. She stopped kendo after getting married and having children, but started again after an 18 year break. Six months after restarting, she was successful in the 3-dan examination. Now working as a nurse, she trains at the dojo two times a week.

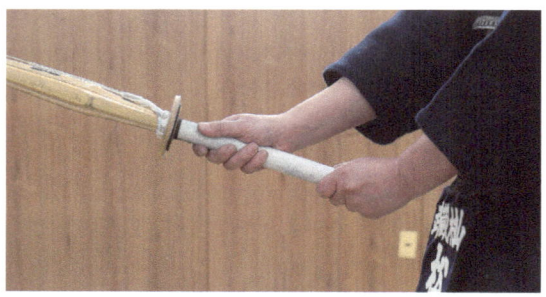

Matsudaira-san's previous kamae. The right thumb is placed directly on top of the shinai, and the fingers and thumb are separated.

After having her kamae fixed, the thumb is in the right position, and the fingers are connected. This greatly improved the power of her strikes.

Hatano-sensei's grip. The palm of the hand is completely wrapped around the tsuka, the right thumb is pointing inwards with the thumbnail pointing about 1-1.5m forward.

ONLY LOTS OF PRACTICE MAKES PERFECT

When you are unable to do *keiko* for a while due to family circumstances, work, or other reasons, what can be done to keep your kendo level up? As long as you are not ill or injured, you can always do *suburi*. Actually, you can practise *suburi* on your own, and learn such things as how to use your side muscles and your left hand. You can check your *kamae* in a mirror or your reflection in the window, and imitate the *kamae* of a teacher that your respect. These are all important training activities that you can do on your own. The most important thing though, is to use this opportunity to reflect on your own kendo, and analyse it flaws and all. This can be done through reading. For example, translations of classic kendo books, and of course, *Kendo World* are treasure troves for information to help you improve. It is important to read books that reflect the importance of human hardship as this will help guide and motivate you as you develop your kendo.

The Left Hand

Let's now take a look at the left hand. Given its connection with the left side of the body, the left knee, and left lower back, proper use of the left hand is paramount in kendo. The left armpit should be lightly closed. In the old days, kendo sensei used to advise that the left armpit should be closed just enough to prevent a sheet of paper falling out. This basically means that the armpit should not be closed too tightly, nor should it be open too much. If the left armpit is closed with just enough tightness, the centre region of the shoulders will not move when you strike. It will enable the left leg to cock adequately as there will be a degree of tautness behind the left knee, but the leg will bend if the left armpit is too open.

The position of the left hand is related to the left armpit. It is taught that the left hand should be situated one fist away from the body. However, if the left hand is put in this position, the left armpit will almost always open up. If the left hand is not positioned approximately two fists in front of the body, it will be impossible to lightly close the left armpit. By placing the left hand two fists in front, your whole left side will expand and straighten up. This means that you will appear bigger to your opponent. If the left hand moves when in *kamae*, this is an indication that your left armpit is open. Closing it will stabilise your left hand.

People who are good at *shiai* or athletically coordinated are able to load their weight on their right foot and respond appropriately to the opponent's attacks. One of my students, Hayafuji Hiromi, is a gifted competitor who has participated in the National Housewives Tournament. She had a habit of loading her weight on the front foot, and was particularly adept at stepping back to strike *kote-nuki-men*. This technique worked well for her, but is not effective against people with higher grades. Whenever I applied pressure on her, she would jump back in a way that I refer to as "shrimp kendo". This can be fixed by pushing the left hand forward more.

* Hayafuji Hiromi's Experience

"Since learning to shift my weight to the back foot, I feel more freedom in my movement and am able to attack with more ease. Hatano-sensei suggested that if I felt different than before then I am on the right track. As I had taken quite a long break away from kendo, I decided to start from zero and rethink my way of doing kendo. This has made me a lot more aware, and I can approach my *keiko* with more clarity."

Hayafuji-san practised kendo for two years at junior high school. She stopped after this and restarted after getting married and having children as a way of releasing stress. She currently trains two or three times a week. She passed 3-dan and 4-dan on her first attempt, and 5-dan on her second attempt. She has also competed at the National Housewives Tournament.

Hayafuji-san's former kamae (top) was front heavy. She placed her weight on the front foot to enable rapid backward movement. By positioning the left hand further in front, her armpit closed, and her overall kamae was more balanced (bottom).

By placing more emphasis on the position of the left hand and closing the left armpit, the kensen will naturally point towards the opponent's solar plexus.

Lowering the kensen will create more spring in the left hand. This will make the overhead swing sharper.

The *shinai* should be held from above with both hands. The *tsuru* should line up with the V between the thumb and forefinger of both hands. The little finger of the left hand should be positioned over the end of the butt of the *tsuka* to keep the *shinai* stable and in hand when striking. Also, be sure to put more strength in the grip with your little finger and ring finger. If the left armpit is closed and the left hand is two fists in front, the *kensen* will end up in a good position. Of course, this should be adjusted to suit the height of your opponent.

It is often mentioned that the *kensen* should point to the opponent's left eye, or should be at throat height. I suspect, however, that people feel that this is a little too high. I prefer to keep my *kensen* pointing at my opponent's solar plexus. There are various reasons for this. The first is to convey my will to the person standing in front of me. Holding the *kensen* at this height is an effective way of channelling one's willpower and applying pressure. Furthermore, if your *kensen* is too high, it will result in weaker striking. Try fighting with your *kensen* in a higher position than the throat or left eye. You can probably strike men without needing to lift the *shinai* overhead, but it will never generate an appropriate amount of power. Keeping the left hand two fists in front and lowering the *kensen* slightly will tighten the top of the wrist. This will in turn give your *kensen* more zing, more latent power, and a stronger strike.

Obituary
Inoue Yoshihiko
1928–2015

Philosopher, Historian, Author, Kendo Teacher

By Graham Sayer

Inoue Hanshi passed away on April 11, 2015. Inoue-sensei was awarded 8-dan in 1977 and was bestowed the title of Hanshi in 1987. He believed deeply in the power of true kendo to develop love, mutual respect and peace in the world. He spoke and wrote of his experiences as a prison guard for death row prisoners. The conversations he had with men that only had a matter of minutes left on this earth in many ways helped form his view on how to live.

Inoue Hanshi also spoke and wrote of his experiences of doing kendo for a living. At one stage in his career, the more *shiai* he won, the higher his salary was.

In recent times, however, Inoue Hanshi spoke of his concern for the future of kendo and the fact that it was evolving into a stick fighting exercise in some quarters, instead of its true purpose: developing the human spirit. When Sensei thought that the message was not getting through verbally, he wrote it down—sometimes whole books! In my case, he gave me a beautifully hand-written letter of advice after a recent failure, as well as arranging for an academic fellow kenshi at the dojo to help me understand it.

Inoue Hanshi had an uncanny ability to speak to the complete dojo after *keiko* and you would swear he was directing the talk at you. I was so convinced of this I started questioning other kenshi after practice; almost everyone left thinking they had been spoken to directly (sometimes in a very harsh manner but somehow filled with compassion).

I wrote this obituary some months after the original version which was for the *Kendo World* website. I wish to say that initially the void left by not having Sensei present at every *keiko* has transformed itself into a feeling of collective determination by Chion Kenshukan members

to not let the "Inoue Hanshi Way" fade. The focus is not to do kendo just to see if you can beat someone, but to practise with the intent to develop as a human being along with your fellow kendoka. Some evidence of this surge in determination has resulted in three dojo members successfully passing 7-dan in the last few months, bringing the total number of 7-dan at Chion Kenshukan to 16 from a pool of around 55 members

Inoue Hanshi always had an open door policy for anyone to come and practise kendo at Chion Kenshukan, regardless of grade, gender, or race. This is the way he wished all dojo to be worldwide. His ability to understand how kendo feels or looks to non-Japanese speakers always amazed me, and has taught me that kendo is so much more than a "traditional Japanese martial art", but more of a way of life to be shared by everyone willing to put the effort in.

Inoue-sensei is survived by his wife, son, daughter, five grandchildren, and four great grandchildren.

R.I.P. Inoue Hanshi

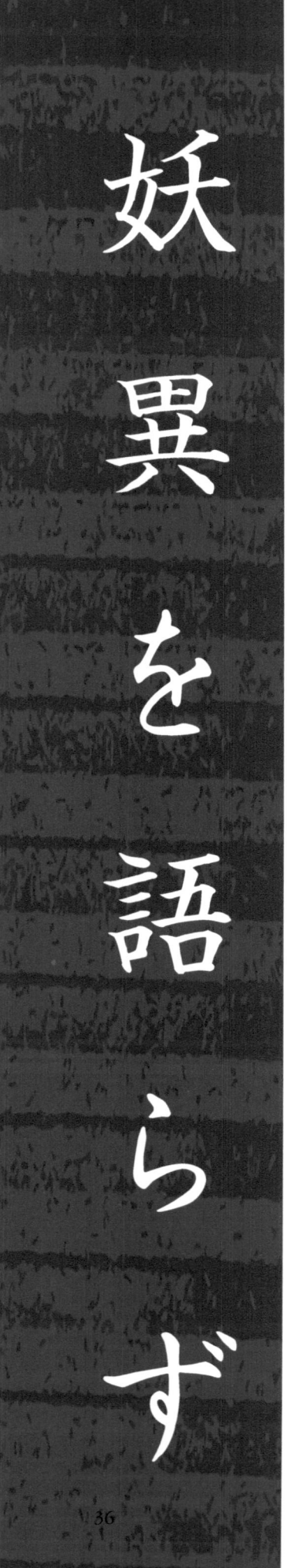

妖異を語らず

"Yōi wo katarazu"
("Don't dwell on the mystery")

Sekiguchi Ujinari (1636–1716) developed the Sekiguchi-ryū after inheriting his father's teachings.

Battle in medieval Japan was never as clear cut as it is often depicted. Warriors needed to be adaptable, and skilled in various combat techniques. A warrior might start in a frenzied exchange of thrusting with a long, pointy *yari* (spear), followed by tussling at close quarters with a dagger, and then grappling his opponent. Different battle scenarios called for different weapons, and early *bujutsu* schools were often multifaceted and included an array of weaponry. Schools often associated with the art of swordsmanship also emphasised many different weapons—*naginata*, *shuriken*, *jūjutsu*, *yari*...

Similarly schools of *jūjutsu*—unarmed grappling—specialised in much more than hand-to-hand combat. A *jūjutsu* exponent knew how to use different weapons as a matter of course. It was not until the peaceful Tokugawa period that comprehensive schools of weaponry became segregated. Until then, it was in everybody's best interest to keep one's repertoire diverse.

A good example of this can be seen in the Sekiguchi-ryū, one of the so-called four great schools of *jūjutsu*. The founder was the famous Sekiguchi Ujimune (aka Jūshin). A dedicated martial artist, Sekiguchi left the confines of his castle and headed for the Atago Mountains where he engaged in a rigorous regime of physical and spiritual training. Experiencing an epiphany in the mountains, he then formulated his own school of *jūjutsu*, which became known as Sekiguchi Shinshin-ryū, and his fame spread throughout the provinces. Even though his school is known as a grappling tradition, he incorporated sword drawing techniques which he learned from Hayashizaki

SWORDS OF WISDOM

By
ALEX BENNETT
Based on the book
"KENSHI NO MEIGON" (1998)
by the late Tobe Shinjūrō
Used with author's permission.

Jinsuke, and grappling methods influenced by Miura Yoshiuemon. He also included spear and staff techniques, horsemanship, and of course, *kenjutsu*. So famous did he become, he was appointed as a teacher for the Kishū domain by Tokugawa Yorinobu. Even the eighth shogun, Tokugawa Yoshimune, became a licensed teacher of the school.

One of many famous episodes surrounding the incredible skill of Ujimune involves cats. One day when he was in the garden, he saw a cat fall from a tree but it somehow managed to spin midair just enough to land on all fours. Impressed by this magnificent display of dexterity, Ujimune trained himself to be able to withstand any force applied to his body and remain perfectly balanced. A true copycat.

His successor was his son, Sekiguchi Ujinari. Ujinari was in no way less eccentric that his father. In fact, given his penchant for ridiculously ostentatious clothes, and the impossibly long 1.5m sword propped up with little wheels on the *kojiri* of the scabbard to keep it from dragging on the ground, he was perhaps even more so. Not satisfied to rest on his father's wealth and reputation, he set out to make a name for himself and ended up in the service of Lord Sanada of the Shinshū Matsushiro domain.

His lord asked Ujinari, "I hear that true masters of the martial arts have superhuman powers that enable them to move through walls. How is this so?" Ujinari replied, "Hmmm, give me some food and drink and I'll tell you." Suitably fed, Ujinari then decided to enlighten his benefactor. "The only way to excel in the martial arts is to discard your ego and throw yourself into training. It is not about learning to fool enemies with dubious tricks. Why is it that people insist on explaining the feats of great men like my father, or Tsukahara Bokuden, as mysterious or magical? Disappearing into a wall, could be nothing more than digging under it, or finding a suitably sized hole! Ladders are pretty useful, too. There is no need to dwell on the mystery, as it just belittles the hard work of a master. A man of stature like yourself should be wary of such baloney, and certainly not seek it… In my humble opinion. Sire… Howz about another drink?"

It was probably not the answer Lord Sanada was hoping for, but it is hard to argue against. Ujinari's pragmatism is highlighted by his audacious request for nourishment before imparting this irrefutable wisdom. Even the legendary swordsman Tsukahara Bokuden supposedly said, "Upon seeing the sublime skill of another, those who cannot perform such exploits are only too quick to attribute it to special powers." Being beguiled by mystery is not so much testament to the cosmic supremacy of the master, but more confirmation of the lack of skill and training in the beholder. Students of the earliest schools were subjected to secret rituals and religious teachings to overcome the fear of death, and they even studied divination to attain a magical advantage in battle. As a master of *jūjutsu* and *kenjutsu*, though, Ujinari was far more pragmatic in his approach. He avoided falling into the trap of believing in intangible special powers and relying on superstitions. To him, it was just a matter of training. Nothing more, nothing less.

REI
DAN

The Greater Meaning of Kendo

JI

CHI

REIDAN-JICHI PART 19
WAZA BASICS

By Prof. Ōya Minoru (Kendo Kyōshi 7-dan)
International Budo University

Translated by Alex Bennett

Harai-waza

Harai-waza is used against opponents who have no openings in their *kamae*. Their *shinai* can be deflected upwards, sideways, or downwards from the left or the right to break the *kamae* and follow up with an attack. If the opponent's *kensen* is firmly planted on your centreline, you cannot strike logically unless it is removed. *Harai-waza* is employed for this purpose.

(1) How to Deflect and Use the Waza

① Deflection

Harai-waza are executed in one curved movement rather than two straight movements. In other words, the deflection and strike should be executed as one movement rather than two. After deflecting the opponent's *shinai*, your own *shinai* continues on an upward path and flows into the attack. The deflection should be made with the *shinogi* (side) of your *shinai*, around the *monouchi*, against the middle of the opponent's *datotsu-bu* and continue into the overhead swing ready to strike. It is important for the wrists to be flexible in order to do this. As soon as contact is made, the wrists should be used to sharply deflect the opponent's *shinai*.

Two straight movements (bad example)

Opponent's *shinai*

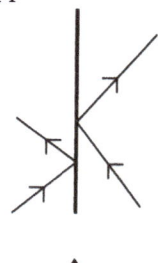

Your *shinai*

One semi-circular movement (good example)

Opponent's *shinai*

Your *shinai*

② Deflecting for the Advantage

If you deflect the opponent's *shinai* to the side to unsettle their *kamae*, take care not to become unbalanced yourself. Over-exerting in the *harai* may leave you in a 50/50 position rather than giving you the advantage where you have an opportunity to strike. Thus, the whole point of *harai* is to ensure that your opponent's *kensen* is removed from your centreline, enabling you to carry through for a strike. Ensure that the technique is executed in a way that you can seize the advantage.

③ Deflect→Strike

Do not think about executing the *harai* and then following up with a strike in a two-step move. As demonstrated in the diagrams, the *harai* should flow into the overhead swing in one seamless movement. It is as if you are attempting to strike, and as you swing the *shinai* overhead, it clears the opponent's *shinai* out of the way inadvertently. Also, if you execute the *harai* with your right hand, not only will it be ineffective, it will also prevent you from making an adequate strike. As you slide forward with your right foot, ensure that your left side and left hand remain stable, and in position. *Harai* is even more effective if you can time it just as the opponent is about to strike or retreat.

(2) Waza

① Omote (Ura) Harai-men

Step out with the right foot as you deflect the opponent's *shinai* to the left (or the right) as you swing up for the strike.

② Ura Harai-kote

Step out with the right foot as you sharply deflect the opponent's *shinai* on the *ura* side (your right) and continue through to strike *kote*.

③ Ura Migi-dō

Step out with the right foot as you sharply deflect the opponent's *shinai* on the *ura* side (your right) and continue through to strike *migi-dō*.

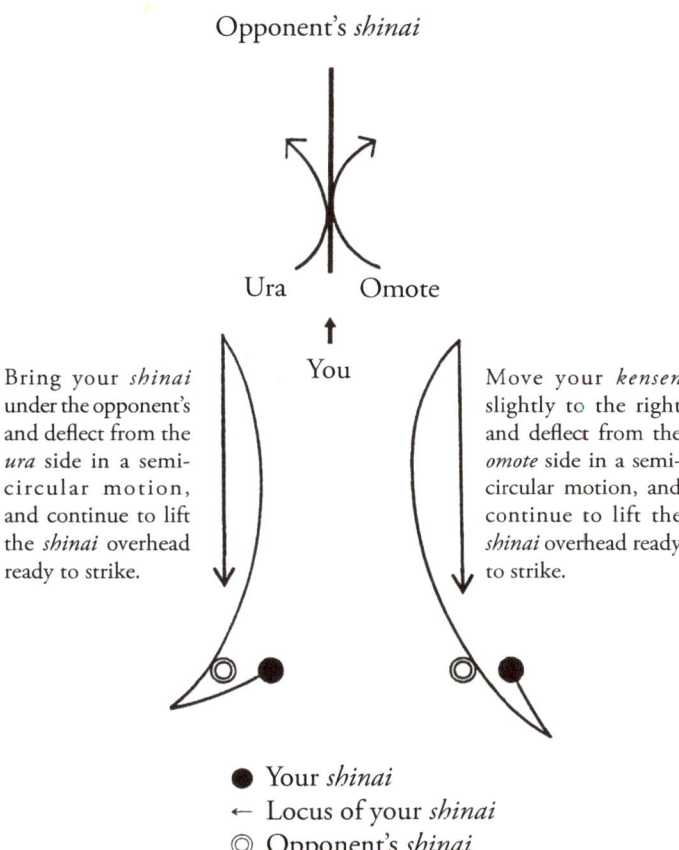

- ● Your *shinai*
- ← Locus of your *shinai*
- ◎ Opponent's *shinai*

\<Points to Take Heed of\>

① The *harai* movement and the striking movement must be combined. Take particular care of the distance and target you are attempting to strike and use your right foot and shinai as smoothly as possible without any extraneous movement.

② When attempting *harai-kote*, the deflection must be made in a small sharp movement.

In the next instalment, I will take a look at *debana-waza*.

BIG TIME GRADING POINTERS

Iwatate Saburō (Kendo Hanshi 8-dan)
Translated by Alex Bennett

The following is a list of things that I am looking for as an examiner in *dan* gradings.

1. Kamae
- Make sure that your posture is upright. Your backside should not be protruding, so try to push your hips forward. Open your chest, straighten your shoulders, and stretch the back of your left knee. This will ensure that your hips and lower back centre your *kamae*.
- Hold your gaze as if you are looking down on your opponent. Imagine you are looking down from a hill.
- If the *monomi* on your *men* is not at eye-level, this will result in you leaning forward slightly in order to see clearly. This in turn will mean that your *men* will be 10cm closer to the opponent, as if you are offering it on a plate. If you have a straight, upright posture, your *men* looks further away from the opponent's perspective, which gives you the advantage.
- Don't create your *kamae* AFTER you stand up from *sonkyo*. Your *kamae* should be ready to go AS you stand up. It's too late if you get *ki*'d up after you stand. You should be replete with energy as you bow in.

2. The right timing
- Everybody in an examination assumes a good *kamae*. If you strike at *kote* while your opponent is standing tall in proper *kamae*, you will not succeed. If you start by striking *kote*, you will fail the examination. This is because you have not yet destabilised your opponent's stance. You can't strike at *kote* unless you have managed to pressure your opponent into raising their hands.
- It is really important to hold your ground and keep applying *seme* until your opponent is unable to hold back. In other words don't jump the gun until the time is right and you have elicited a response.

3. Advice for the oldies
- It is tough for elderly practitioners to pass an examination. So, what can you do to increase your chances? It's all about vitality. In other words, your voice. Bellow out a *kiai* of the loudness and level somebody ten years your junior. Examiners want to see youthfulness.

4. Dō techniques
- You will get full marks if you can draw your opponent out and make them strike *men*, and then counter by striking their *dō*. If your opponent attacks *men* and you react by striking *dō*, this is essentially worthless. Apply *seme*, make him strike at you, and then finish him off with *dō*.
- Your opponent will be aiming for *debana*. Entice him to strike *men*. If you get enticed instead, it's all over.

5. The importance of maai
- Do you know your *maai*? Do you know your optimum distance for striking? You will not be successful if you strike from a half-hearted distance. If you are not able to hit your opponent, this is the reason why.
- Pressure applied from *issoku-ittō-no-maai* is weak. You must enter in a little bit closer. This is your *uchima*, your optimal striking distance.

6. A head above the rest

- Gradings are conducted in groups of four. You have to stand out among the crowd to pass. You have to be more noticeable than the other three. Stand out in terms of your *waza*, spirit, vigour, and mentality.

7. Getting the point

- It is important to get the decisive *ippon*. Don't let your strikes float off into the ether with indecisive, monotone *kiai* "meeeen…meeen" It has to be conclusive. The quality of one devastating strike, not lots of random hits. "Bang!"
- Don't break the connection. Keep the flow going. If you score an *ippon*, and then sever the circuit it will amount to nothing. Always continue into the next phase of attack and defence.

8. Kakegoe

- *Kakegoe* means *kiai*, or vocalization. Let out the loudest yell you can, then another, and then another, and creep even a toenail closer to your opponent. If you do this, he will surely feel the heat. This means you can create your stage.
- Make sure you have the loudest *kiai* in the hall.

9. Sales point

- You will need a technique which will impress the examiners. "Oh yes! This is THE *ippon*!"
- That is to say, you have to score something that resonates in the minds of the examiners.
- Aim for the heart-and-soul strike.

10. Recognition

- Of course, you have to convince the examiners that your *ippon* is valid. So, what kind of techniques leave a lasting impression? *Debana-men*, and *debana-kote*…
- But, you need to make your opponent move to pull these off. Then, nip their move in the bud.
- Calmness under pressure is the key here. Make your opponent rush to take the bait.

11. Hold 'em then fold 'em

- If you score, don't let your opponent turn the tables and score on you. As it is an examination, however, this is not to say that you should dodge your opponent. If you dodge or run away, you're finished. Instead, smother your opponent with your *ki*.
- Use your *shinai* to knock them off balance as they try to move in. Control their *shinai* to the left and right. In other words, don't allow them a chance to strike.
- Score, and hold it without giving the opponent a chance to take it back. If you can demonstrate this ability, then the examiners will be impressed!
- One of the things the examiners are looking for is your competitiveness. If you get struck after you score a point, it nullifies your efforts.
- If you score a point and hold your opponent back, this is a show of supreme confidence, and the examiners will be impressed. If you hold on and control your opponent after scoring, they will start throwing caution to the wind. This will give you even more chances to show your stuff.

12. Don't let your guard down

- Don't relax after scoring. Strike, score, and take the match by the scruff of the neck. If you are on top it will look as though you are controlling your opponent, which makes you seem very strong in the eyes of the examiners.
- If you just keep striking randomly though, you will not seem in control or strong.
- *Zanshin* is the first step for the next attack. The connection between *zanshin* and *seme* must never be broken.

13. In total

In your daily *keiko*, always strike with loud voice. Even if the strike isn't good, continue going through as if it is. Make every strike with commitment and decisiveness, and keep the momentum going.

Obituary
Mochizuki Teruo
1945–2015

Kendo Teacher
Business Leader
All-Rounder

By Graham Sayer

Mochizuki Teruo-sensei died on June 29, 2015. Mochizuki-sensei was Kendo Kyōshi 8-dan, and President of the Shizuoka Kendo Federation from 2013 until his death. Unfortunately, my time knowing Mochizuki-sensei was relatively short (just five years). I can honestly say that I have never met such a highly graded kendo master with so many interests outside of the kendo world that he took very seriously. These include, but are not limited to:

Gardening: He was especially fond of English style gardens, and he pursued this hobby with his wife. Their home garden in Fuji City was used on a number of occasions as a show garden for other enthusiasts.

European and Japanese antiques: Sensei's home was like a small museum, and when I accompanied him on two overseas trips (NZ and China), I found myself assisting him in bargaining at antique shops in both countries.

Marine sports: It is very unusual to find a man of Mochizuki-sensei's era who can surf and sail a yacht. I took him kayaking in 2012 with a group of beginners and he picked it up faster than some people 40 years his junior.

Zazen: Perhaps more than a "hobby", he referred to his practice of Zen a lot over the past two years, and I sensed it was of great help to him as he battled cancer.

I have referred to Mochizuki-sensei as an "all-rounder". The Japanese use this phrase when describing a person and the way he or she lives life; not just as a way to describe sporting expertise.

A dedicated family man, Sensei always spoke with pride and love in regards to his family; one of his daughters and three grandchildren practise kendo.

He conducted his business empire in the same way he did kendo. He stuck to basics (*kihon*), planned carefully, and presented in the best possible way with nothing less that 100% effort. His company dojo boasts two 8-dan and five 7-dan instructors in its teaching ranks.

This photo was taken in 2013 outside an antique shop in Ponsonby, Auckland. Mochizuki-sensei is wearing an antique NZ farming jacket, a Swanndri, he had just purchased.

Mochizuki-sensei's funeral presented his life well and the huge contribution he made to other people's lives. The photo that is displayed at a person's funeral is carefully selected as it needs to show as much as possible about the subject. The photo chosen for his funeral was indeed a moment in time where he looked happy and content. This photo had a special connection to me, and I hope it went a little way toward repaying Sensei for what he gave me in encouragement, teaching, and advice over the short time that I knew him. He is survived by his wife, son, two daughters, and seven grandchildren.

R.I.P. Mochizuki Teruo Sensei

Walking in the Footsteps of The Exceptional Charles Boxer

By Paul Budden

On 11 March, 1930, a young lieutenant in the British Army arrived in Kobe and boarded a train for Tokyo as part of a three-year programme of exchange between Japanese and English officers. His position was that of a language officer, and he became an interpreter in Japanese translating for high ranking officers, even on occasion for members of the Japanese imperial family. He remained in Tokyo for one year of intensive language instruction until his attachment in 1931 to the 38th Japanese Infantry regiment (38th Hohei Rentai) based in Nara. Further assignments at the Toyohasi Noncommissioned Officers training school also followed. This officer would, however, become much more than a mere translator and his accomplishments would come to include the practice of kendo. Extensive travel within Japan and throughout the Far East played a major part in his development during this period. An unquenchable thirst for historical research and a consuming desire to write would continue throughout his lifetime.
The officer's name was Charles Ralph Boxer.

Charles Ralph Boxer, a British kendo pioneer, is the subject of a new book *'The Silent Patient' —An English Samurai: The Exceptional Charles Boxer (1904 – 2000)*, due to be published by Kendo World/Bunkasha International in Summer 2015. What follows are some extracts from that book as well as details of my trip to Japan that took in some of the important locations in Boxer's story. During the extensive research that was undertaken in preparation of this book, a great deal of new information about Boxer was unearthed, as well as a Japanese article on Michael Dobbs-Higginson, another foreign kendoka practising in Japan. A Rhodesian by birth, Michael Dobbs-Higginson had studied kendo in 1963 while living in Nara. I was able to make contact with Michael and we first met at our dojo, Kodokan U.K., and this was followed by a "commemorative return" to Nara, as it was called by Michael. This allowed me to visit some of the locations associated with the kendo stories of both Michael Dobbs-Higginson and Charles Boxer.

As mentioned above, Boxer originally came to Japan as a language officer with the British Army.

The picture above (circa 1931) is of Charles Boxer with his 38th Hohei Rentai colleagues, and his sensei, Shimatani Yasohachi, with the Nara Butokuden buildings in the background.

This is the former site of the Nara Butokuden. Although the original site of the Butokuden is now the Nara Prefectural Office, the area in front remains virtually unchanged.

In 1961, the Butokuden building was moved from its original location in the heart of Nara City to Kashihara Park in Kashihara City, Nara prefecture. The original building was unfortunately destroyed in a storm and had to be rebuilt. It is now referred to as the Kashihara Kōen Jūken dojo where both judo and kendo are still practised.

The following quote appears in an article titled "Meeting a British Student", from *Daidō: Kensei Shimatani Yasohachi Sensei* (Kensei Shimatani Happōkai, Matsukasa-chō, 1996), a book about Shimatani Yasohachi-sensei.

"It was perhaps at the beginning of Showa (1926–89) when a U.K. first lieutenant named Boxer, who was sent to the Nara regiment on a mission to research the Japanese military system, was trained intensively for around one year by Shimatani Yasohachi-sensei. He studied kendo very hard and his behaviour gave stimulus and encouragement to the other students of Shimatani-sensei. I visited Boxer's residence, a summer house in Kawanokami Tsukinuke-chō belonging to a Mr. Niimura, several times with Shimatani-sensei. Boxer would ask Shimatani sensei for an expert opinion on his swords and show us his research papers on tsuba—Japanese sword guards."

Through the great kindness and generosity of Uegaki Isao-sensei, who is researching the history of the Nara Kendo Federation, the location of the summer house was pinpointed in Kawanokami Tsukinuke-cho. Unfortunately, the original building had been demolished some years before, but there are still a few remaining old-style Japanese houses identical to the one that Charles Boxer, along with his housekeeper and concubine, would have resided in from 1931–32 directly adjacent to the plot.

"After arriving in Kyoto late in 1931 Boxer located

Kawanokami Tsukinuke-chō

around Kawanokami Tsukinuke-chō, not so far from Takabatake-chō in Nara and probably went to the Butokuden on foot for kendo practice, the distance being around 1.5 km".

I was extremely fortunate to be taken to the Kashihara Kōen Jūken dojo, the former Nara Butokuden, where I was shown around this remarkable building by Hayashi Sadayuki-sensei, the current president of the entire Kashihara Park complex. He is a graduate of Tenri University, another place very much associated with the life and times of Charles Boxer. On September 30, 1931, Boxer visited Tenri University and its library for the first time and in 1991, he made his final visit to Japan, coincidentally to give a lecture at the same university. At that time, he was also taken to visit the hall where, 60 years earlier, he had practised kendo with his colleagues from the 38th infantry regiment. From the pictorial evidence we know this to be the relocated Nara Butokuden in Kashihara City.

Kashihara Koen Ju-ken dojo

Michael Dobbs-Higginson's return to Japan would be the connection of two kindred spirits: himself and Charles Boxer. The first connection between these two men is Nara University of Education. This is where Michael practised kendo in 1963; and it was also the base for the 38th Imperial Army Infantry Regiment (the 38th Hohei Rentai) in 1931—the regiment that Charles Boxer had been seconded to. The second way in which Michael Dobbs-Higginson and Charles Boxer are connected was through the late Murata Kanzo-sensei, the instructor who had taught both foreign students over the span of 32 years.

During his stay in Nara, Michael Dobbs-Higginson also became a Buddhist lay monk, and was ordained under the name Zenku Eison. During our visit to Nara,

Practice at the Nara University of Education dojo

San-Sho-Zenji temple

we went with Michael to San-Sho-Zenji temple and to Shushinkan dojo which had been run by the late Kagita-sensei. Kagita-sensei had also been the Mayor of Nara at the time of Michael's arrival, and was extremely curious as to what this young foreigner might be up to. To find out, he had the police collect him and bring him in for an interview. This resulted in Michael's enrolment into both daily kendo and *zazen*. His kendo education was then taken over shortly after by Murata Kanzo-sensei.

In this short trip to Japan, I feel very honoured to have been included in both Michael's reunion, which was closure for him on his early life in Japan, and to also walk in the footsteps of one of Britain's kendo pioneers—the exceptional Charles Boxer.

Michael Dobbs-Higginson

In addition to Boxer's pre-war kendo experiences, *'The Silent Patient' —An English Samurai: The Exceptional Charles Boxer (1904 – 2000)* will also look at his war-time experiences, which included time in a Japanese POW camp, his academic career and personal life. His story is a remarkable one, of a man whose life straddled two worlds and a turbulent era in history, and gives us a unique perspective of those times.

Uegaki Isao-sensei demonstrates the zazen position

The co-conspirators of the "Charles Boxer Project". Left to right: Matsuda Kazuyo, Paul Budden, Alex Bennett, Nagao Susumu. Not present was Charles Boxer's daughter, the actress Amanda Boxer, who also made a great contribution to this project.

Shushinkan dojo, Nara

Bujutsu Jargon Part 7

Reference guide covering various bujutsu-related terminology

Bruce Flanagan MA
Lecturer - Tokyo University of Science

#45 克己 kokki

To 'triumph over the self'. The first character is *katsu* (to win/conquer) and the second is *onore* (oneself). *Kokki* refers to controlling one's impulses/desires/feelings with the strength of one's *ishi* (willpower). A spirit of discipline or self-control is called *kokki-shin* (克己心). Other similar terms referring to self-control include *jisei-shin* (自制心) and *jiko-yokusei* (自己抑制). A sense of cultivated refinement and selfless courtesy is *kokki-fukurei* (克己復礼).

#46 禅 zen

Zen, in it's Japanese form, is an adjunct practice of Buddhism, generally involving meditation in order to achieve religious enlightenment (*satori*) and was introduced to Japan from China in the 12th century. Practitioners often perform *zazen* (座禅), or seated meditation, by stilling the mind, controlling breathing, and maintaining a relaxed level of concentration free of conscious thought. Zen was popular amongst Japanese warriors who constantly faced the threat of death. Practitioners can apply the Zen skill of meditative concentration known as *zenjō* (禅定) to their everyday life.

#47 受け身 ukemi

The verb *ukeru* means to 'be passive' or to 'receive' and *mi* means body. *Ukemi* is therefore the state when your opponent moves or initiates an attack first and you are forced to make a delayed response. This will often mean being on the receiving-end of an attack or throw. In arts such as judo and aikido which feature many *nage-waza* (throwing techniques), *ukemi* generally refers to making a defensive motion or assuming a posture to minimize impact damage with the ground such as break-falling or rolling.

#48 急所 kyūsho

Are the vital points or targets of the body which are vulnerable or susceptible to attack and may incur severe damage or life-threatening injury if forcefully struck. Many martial artists train to target the *kyūsho* of their opponent, such as the groin, nose, eyes, ears, neck or throat, but other *kyūsho* may include internal organs, bones, arteries, veins, or pressure points (*tsubo*).

#49 八幡神 hachiman-jin

The deity spirit of combat and archery to whom warriors prayed or swore an oath to in ancient times. Considered the 'god of war', warriors would often utter the name Hachiman to invoke the deity's assistance when under pressure. The *hachiman-jin* spirit is said to be a deification of the semi-legendary Japanese emperor Ōjin of the 3rd and 4th centuries. *Hachiman-jin* is also known as *yawata-no-kami* and was traditionally a guardian spirit of the Minamoto clan. The popular deity has an enormous following in modern times and continues to be worshipped in shrines known as *hachiman-gū* (八幡宮).

#50 気合 kiai

A broad term which literally means 'union of energy' *kiai* has many subtle connotations. The main purpose of *kiai* is the increase in physical and mental power produced by focusing one's entire self on a task. The second meaning of *kiai*, which is an extension of the first, is the vocalization or grunt of exertion (either voluntary and involuntary), that often accompanies this act of extreme focus. The cries or yells of modern budo arts are a form of *kiai*, but the more correct term is *kake-goe* (掛け声). Therefore it is technically possible to perform *kiai* in complete silence, because the vocalization is merely an aid to, or a result of, the *kiai* process. Nonetheless, the practice of vocalization for mental focus is called *kiai-jutsu* (気合術). Historically, a battlefield cry to brace troops for engagement or to frighten the enemy was called *toki-no-koe* (鬨の声). To be psychologically defeated by an opponent's strong presence and lose one's power or aggression before a fight or competition is called *kiai-make* (気合負け).

#51 風水 fūsui

Is the Japanese pronunciation of the term for the traditional Chinese practice of *feng shui*. The term is comprised of the two characters for wind (*kaze*) and water (*mizu*). *Feng shui* is a metaphysical belief system which, among other applications, sets out standards for the location, positioning and construction of castles, homes, temples, graves or other such buildings based on the principles of *yin* and *yang* (*in-yō* in Japanese). *Feng shui* will generally take into the account the locations of nearby mountains and rivers and consider the flow of water and *ki* energy through the surrounding landscape. The practice is used to increase the good fortune or prosperity (*en*) of the site and is occasionally still seen in the planning and construction of martial arts dojos in Japan.

Bibliography

- *Bujutsu Jiten (Zusetsu)*, Osano J., Shinkigensha, 2003.
- *Kōjien (Daigohan)*, Iwanami Shoten, 2004.
- *Hachiman*, Ultimate Reference Suite, Encyclopaedia Britannica, 2008.
- *Nihon Budō Jiten (Zusetsu)*, Sasama Y., Kashiwa-Shobō, 2003.

Hagakure and "Sutemi"

by Alex Bennett

In my previous article, I presented a brief outline of *Hagakure*, a classic treatise on bushido written in the early eighteenth century by samurai of the Saga domain in the southern Japanese island of Kyushu. I mentioned how *Hagakure* wisdom was often greatly misunderstood, but with contextualisation, it serves as a fascinating window on the trials and tribulations of the samurai lifestyle in a time of tense, but prevailing peace in Pax Tokugawa. *Hagakure* was completed in 1716, and this was a time in which the martial arts (*bugei*) were undergoing a significant transformation in terms of form, objective, philosophy, and rationale. The glory of battle was a distant memory for most, but the importance of overcoming fear of death remained a central concern in the warrior ethos. This remained interwoven in the theoretical fabric of the martial arts even though the form in which they were practised was continually evolving.

In this sense, although rarely associated directly with martial arts practice per se, many of the dictums in *Hagakure* provide an intriguing backdrop to key concepts espoused in the modern Japanese martial arts (budo). One such concept is that of "*sutemi*." Literally to "discard one's body," this is the mental and physical state of total commitment in giving something one's all, even to the extent of giving up one's life if need be. In budo, this amounts to attempting a single blow with all one's force during a bout or exchange, without being concerned with surviving. In essence, it is to execute each technique with self-sacrificial drive and indifference to personal safety. No warrior was more fearsome, samurai believed, than one who cared not for his own life in the thick of battle.

Yamamoto Jōchō's grave stone

The pages of *Hagakure* abound with teachings pointing to the importance of this mind-set in daily life. For example, "'If a samurai steps out of his house, he will be in the midst of corpses; if he steps out of his gate, he will meet the enemy.' The point here is not vigilance; but rather to kill one's self from the very outset." (Book 11–133) In other words, the author is advocating that a samurai should accept the notion that he could be killed at any moment. To hide from this fact would leave him spiritually incapacitated, and unable to respond in an emergency. If he had already sacrificed himself before he left his home, what else did he have to fear? Or, "A heroic warrior (*kusemono*) does not concern himself with victory

A monument to Yamamoto Jōchō near the site of his hermitage in the hills of Saga

or defeat. Without hesitating, he whips himself into a deadly fury (*shini-gurui*). This is when he understands; this is when he awakens from the dream." (1–55) In this case, the stalwart warrior finds spiritual liberation by detaching himself from concerns of winning or losing. Ultimately, he will prevail over others who are more 'calculated' in their approach to gaining a favourable result.

One of my favourite anecdotes demonstrating this point concerns a party of blind monks attempting to traverse a treacherous mountain pass. "Once, there was a group of ten blind monks walking through the mountains. As they passed around the top of a cliff, their legs began to tremble, and although they took extreme care, they were overcome by fear. The leader staggered and then fell off the edge. The rest all cried, 'Oh what a terrible end!' They were unable to take a step further. The blind monk who had fallen off the cliff yelled up from below: 'Do not be frightened. Falling was not so bad. I am now quite unperturbed. I worried about what would happen if I fell, and was somewhat apprehensive. But now I am very calm. If you want to put your minds at ease, quickly fall [and get it over with].'" (10–125)

Sutemi is the requisite mental attitude in all budo in which the adept ideally commits body and soul into the attack in an act of total self-denial and sacrifice, with no concern for the aftermath. What will be, will be. This attitude held the key to the 'Holy Grail' of combat – a superlative combination of body, mind and technique which made the warrior invincible in battle both technically and spiritually through a supposed transcendence of concerns for life and death.

Although nobody fights with bows and arrows, swords or spears anymore, such philosophical and spiritual underpinnings remain an important feature in all budo, which maintain intrinsic connections with the samurai ethos and battlefields of old. Although the forms are considerably different now, the world of modern budo is a precious legacy left by samurai warriors who were encouraged in their training to try and confront their mortality at every living moment. Their accrued wisdom can provide modern practitioners with fantastic insights into the beauty of life, and how to live to one's full potential, paradoxically based on the *sutemi* ideal of self-annihilation. *Hagakure* demonstrates this point beautifully.

J-Concepts' Samurai Green Tea

Samurai Green Tea

Traditional Green Tea from Makinohara City, Shizuoka Prefecture, Japan

ADVERTISEMENT

The Samurai Green Tea Fundraising System

No matter how much we love kendo, the costs involved in it can at times put a strain on even the deepest of wallets. Buying a quality set of *bōgu* can require a big financial commitment, and we've all spent good money on a *shinai* only for it to break after a few training sessions. Even greater are the costs involved in travelling to major competitions.

With the exception of kendoka from the major kendo countries such as Japan, Korea, many competitors receive little or no financial support from their federations and will have to largely pay their own way to compete in major competitions like the WKC. In order to help meet the costs of travel, some competitors or federations will undertake activities like sponsored *suburi-athons*. It is also difficult for small clubs and federations to purchase the equipment necessary to carry out their activities. With these issues in mind, J-Concepts and Kendo World have collaborated to bring you the Samurai Green Tea Fundraising System to help you raise money for your club, federation or competition travel expenses.

So what exactly is the Samurai Green Tea Fundraising System and how can it help you?

First, Samurai Green Tea comes from Makinohara City in Shizuoka prefecture. This is the heart of Japan's "tea country", and is an area synonymous with the finest green tea. Strongly linked to kendo, this tea actually comes from plantations founded by samurai-cum-tea grower, Chūjō Kageaki, whose fascinating story is in the following pages. One canister of Samurai Green Tea contains 20 freshly-packed teabags that can be used to make hot or cold tea. You would order a minimum of one pack of 24 canisters of Samurai Green Tea for $312, which includes postage to anywhere in the world. This works out to be $13 per canister. Next, sell them at the RRP of $19.95, and the profit you make can then go towards paying for travelling expenses, new club *bōgu*, or whatever it is that you need to raise money for.

Seito Kenyukai Original Label

A unique feature of this product is that you are able to personalise it. Create your own label from scratch or use one of our templates. Once you have placed an order and submitted the label artwork, the tea will be picked and packed, and then labels will be affixed to the canisters. You will receive your totally original canisters of Samurai Green Tea 10–20 days later.

1. Contact Graham, your tea and fundraising consultant, at tea@kendo-world.com to see how Samurai Green Tea can help you realise your goal.

2. Design your own label to the required size.

2. Choose one of the many templates and decide what text or photos to use.

3. Submit the label data with your order* and make payment.
    * A minimum order is one carton (24 canisters of 20 tea-bags for $312 including postage to anywhere in the world).

4. Once payment is received, labels will be printed and affixed to canisters.

5. Your tea will then be freshly packed, off the tree not the shelf.

6. Once your product is ready it will be dispatched by international courier.

7. Your carton of customised canisters of tea will arrive 10 to 20 days after confirmation of order depending on your zone. (Delivery times to South America and Africa will take slightly longer.)

8. Sell at the RRP of $19.95 to make $166.80 per carton towards your goal!

9. Still need to raise more funds?

10. No. Buy more tea because it tastes great!

10. Yes. Then buy more tea!

Of course, Samurai Green Tea need not only be bought for fundraising. It can also be used as a commemorative gift to give to friends or family.

Members of Canterbury Kendo Club that were selected to represent New Zealand at the 16th WKC in Tokyo used the Samurai Green Tea Fundraising System to help finance their trip to Japan. Here's what they had to say about it:

"The Samurai Green Tea was a low cost and hugely beneficial aspect of our fundraising efforts to get to the 16th WKC. The option to customise the label made it simple to sell to club members, family and friends. Additionally, as it is green tea, people needed little convincing of its practical value in comparison to other fund raising items we were selling."—Blake Bennett

"Fundraising has always been a tricky one for the kendo club. Over the years and various WKC campaigns, inevitably the same friends and family get asked for money or labour at various sausage sizzles and suburi-athons etc. This time, it was really nice to be able to offer them something back for their support. Even better, something relevant to kendo with the custom label and link to Japanese culture. And it's really good tea, too. A great fundraising tool that we will certainly be using again."—David Wong

So, why not ease the financial burden on your club or federation and partake in the samurai legacy at the same time? If you are cold, Samurai Green Tea will warm you. If you are too hot, it will cool you. If you are depressed, it will cheer you. If you are excited, it will calm you. Each cup of Samurai Green Tea represents an imaginary voyage. It is liquid wisdom with all of the health benefits Japanese green tea is famous for. Samurai Green Tea is the real deal.

Samurai Green Tea is

- **100% PRODUCED IN JAPAN**
- **100% FREE OF PRESERVATIVES OR ADDITIVES**
- **100% ORIGINAL**
- **100% READY FOR DOJO FUNDRAISING**
- **100% PERSONALISED TO USE AS A QUALITY GIFT FOR ANY OCCASION**
- **100% DELICIOUS AND HEALTHY**

Contact Graham, your tea and fundraising consultant, at tea@kendo-world.com to see how he can help you raise money for your federation or club.

contact us **tea@kendo-world.com**   about **http://www.j-conceptsjapan.com/samurai-tea/**

J-Concepts 1082-1 Ieyama Kawane-cho, Shimada-shi, Shizuoka, 428-0104 JAPAN Tel.: +81 (0)80-3689-5978

SWORDS AND TEAPOTS
THE REMARKABLE STORY OF CHŪJŌ KAGEAKI

"A true warrior, like tea, shows his strength in hot water"

Chūjō Kinnosuke Kageaki (1827-1896) was a paragon of greatness whose exploits bridged two epochs in Japanese history. A stalwart samurai and master swordsman of the feudal age, he was destined to become an entrepreneur extraordinaire in the modern era.

A direct retainer of the Tokugawa shogunate, Chūjō learned several styles of swordsmanship including Yamaga-ryū and Tamiya-ryū from the eminent master Kubota Sugane, and was even appointed instructor of kendo at the shogunate's military academy, the Kobushō. He also studied Shingyōtō-ryū, Hokushin Ittō-ryū, and learned Ittō Shōden Mutō-ryū under the tutelage of legendary Meiji statesman and swordsman, Yamaoka Tesshū. All of these schools produced some of Japan's most accomplished swordsmen, many of whom would play a prominent part in the creation of modern kendo.

As a trusted vassal of the shogun, Chūjō was in the thick of the action during the turbulent *bakumatsu* era. Many samurai were outraged that the shogunate had buckled to foreign pressure to open Japanese ports. Under the slogan *"sonnō jōi"* (Revere the emperor, expel the barbarians) a growing number of subversive loyalist samurai sought to restore imperial rule and the end of over seven centuries of warrior hegemony. During this violent period, Chūjō served as one of the directors of the Rōshigumi, a select group of *rōnin* recruited to protect shogun Tokugawa Iemochi's procession from Edo to Kyoto to engage in "a wee chat" with the emperor in 1863.

Nevertheless, once set in motion the tide of change was to prove unstoppable. One of the most significant events in Japanese history, the Meiji Restoration of 1867-1868 brought an end to the Tokugawa shogunate and samurai rule, replacing it with an imperial government under the Emperor Meiji. The Meiji period saw dramatic social change and unbridled adoption of Western technology and ideals as Japan embarked on a frantic quest to modernise. Class distinctions were subsequently dismantled, and the status of samurai existed no more. Tokugawa Yoshinobu was the last shogun. Given no part to play in the Meiji government, he retired to Shizuoka with many of his vassals, as his ancestor Tokugawa Ieyasu did centuries before, and the trusty Chūjō headed his corps of bodyguards as he made his way there.

Reclassified as *"shizoku"* in 1869, the government gave stipends to former samurai to make the transition from privileged class to ordinariness less excruciating. However, due to the massive financial burden on the nation's coffers, *shizoku* were eventually forced to exchange their stipends for government bonds in 1876, leading to the impoverishment of many. Although a considerable number were able to re-establish themselves in new careers—91 percent of Meiji political leaders were from samurai stock, as were 70 percent of cultural leaders, and 23 percent of business leaders—most of them lacked any tangible skills to prosper in the modern age. Many invested their meagre stipends into establishing family companies, but lacking any real business acumen, scores of *shizoku* start-up enterprises failed miserably, leaving once proud samurai broke and destitute.

Chūjō's story, however, is one of heart-warming success. Aged 42, and without any meaningful prospects of employment, he eventually settled in the undeveloped region of Makinohara. Even with no previous experience in agriculture, he was astute enough to recognize the potential for exporting tea and silk. Encouraged by his mentors, the Meiji luminaries Yamaoka Tesshū and Katsu Kaishū, he and his former charges committed themselves to carving out a tea plantation in the barren hills of Makinohara. The families of 250 former shogunate retainers accompanied him on this ambitious undertaking, and together they prepared a 1,425 hectare site for cultivation. Prior to his arrival, green tea was the reserve of only the wealthy, with most of the premium tea being cultivated in Kyoto and its surrounding areas. Because of his foresight, charismatic demeanour, and ability to convince others that there was green gold in those Makinohara hills, the region was turned into Japan's preeminent tea producing locality. The tea plantation now covers about 5,000 hectares, accounting for 10 percent of all tea fields in Japan.

Chūjō is still revered as a hero in the region for his keen business sense and success in creating an enduring tea producing industry, which is now the pride of Shizuoka prefecture. While he was growing tea, he actively engaged in his other passion, kendo, and was an immensely popular teacher with an undying willingness to teach it to all comers. Testament to his importance and influence in the area, visitors to nearby Shimada City's train station can see a statue of Chūjō proudly gazing out over the vast region that he turned into the tea mecca of Japan.

Obituary
Terry Holt
1939–2015

Open-Hearted Enthusiastic Kendo Teacher Mentor

By Geoff Salmon

On January 12 this year, Terry Holt-sensei passed away. In kendo we have the motto "*kōken-chiai*", which loosely translates as "loving your fellow man through the application of the sword". To me, this sums up Terry Holt-sensei's approach to life. Terry will be remembered as one of the founding fathers of British kendo, and one of the first few to gain 7-dan, but above all it was his generosity and kindness to others that set him apart.

Terry was born in London in 1939, just before the outbreak of the Second World War. He lived with his mother and sisters in West Kensington. At the age of seven he discovered a bomb detonator which exploded, causing the loss of his right index finger. In spite of this, he eagerly started judo classes at the age of 10, training regularly until he was bitten by the kendo bug in the late 1960s and joined Nenriki Dojo in London.

He met his wife Gill on a holiday in Cornwall. They married in 1959, settling in Southall, West London. Terry spent the rest of his life in the house he bought with Gill, raising three children, Christine, Wendy and David, and proudly becoming grandfather to seven, and great-grandfather to 10. Terry worked as an electrical engineer, taking on a wide range of projects from appliance repair to sound and lighting for concerts.

In 1968 he became one of the founding members of Mumeishi Kendo Club, establishing the club with the guidance of Fujii Okimitsu and assuming the role of *kanchō* in 1971. The club thrived and today has sister clubs in Melbourne, Tel-Aviv and Tehran. Terry hosted the first Mumeishi 3s Taikai in 1979. This event is now in its 42nd year and continues to attract around 300 competitors from clubs around the globe.

Terry represented Great Britain at the 2nd World Kendo Championships in Los Angeles. As Great Britain's only competitor, he shared a room with Japan's Chiba Masashi-sensei. He was part of the winning G.B. team in the 1974 European Championships. His career within the British Kendo Team embraced a number of key roles, including National Team Coach, a place on the organising committee for the 3rd WKC, and he was Chair of the British Kendo Association between 1980 and 1981. In 1998 he was presented with the Japan Festival Award for furthering understanding of Japanese culture in the U.K.

In his retirement Terry travelled extensively, teaching seminars in Europe, visiting the Mumeishi sister clubs, and trying for 8-dan in Tokyo. He actively kept in touch with numerous kendo friends around the globe.

Terry always took the view that kendo teaching is also learning, and worked side by side with his students. The last time I saw him was just before his illness when he was happily taking points from people during *jigeiko* while helping them improve their kendo. Although a stickler for correct kendo and etiquette, he was always much happier to encourage rather than criticise, and had the ability to make you feel good about yourself even if you had just failed a grading or lost a *shiai*.

His kindness did not stop in the dojo. The home that he shared with Gill and their family has always been a kendo open house. Visiting *kenshi* and their friends and relatives in need of a bed for the night or longer, have always been welcome.

Terry taught me a number of valuable lessons, not just about kendo but also about life. He was testimony to the fact that life is for living, to the full, to the very end. He taught me about the value of friendship and that the principles of kendo go beyond the walls of the dojo.

He will be missed by kendo friends around the world.

The 43rd Mumeishi 3s International Kendo Championship is being held this year on November 14, 2015, in Holt-sensei's honour. There will be a mixed *kyū/dan* three-person team event, a ladies' championship, and children's competition. More details will be available on the Mumeishi Facebook page nearer the time of the event. Competitors from around the world are welcome.

BOOK REVIEW

MIYAMOTO MUSASHI
A Life in Arms

Review by Jeff Broderick

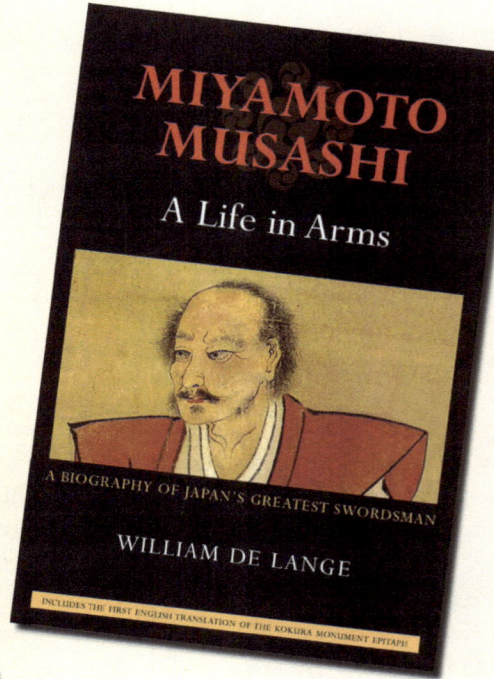

2014, Floating World Editions
$34.95, 254 pages
(including maps, glossary, & index)

Fans of Miyamoto Musashi, who is perhaps Japan's most famous warrior, will know that most discussions of the man begin with, "Actually, very little is known about his life ..." Until recently, that would have been correct.

Historical information about Musashi has always been scant and sometimes contradictory. There has long been confusion, for example, over where he was born, what his original name was, his relationship with his father—even when his most famous duels were fought. However, it turns out that there has been an abundance of material all along in Japanese, which only recently has begun to be translated into English. At the forefront of this activity is William De Lange, a martial artist, writer, and translator who in the past few years has produced the first English translations of two important early biographies of Musashi, the *Bukoden* and *Bushu Denraiki*. Written by students-of-students, these works have been crucial in sweeping away the persistent myths surrounding Musashi's life—myths that came about partly due to the popularity of the novelist Yoshikawa Eiji's fictionalised account of his life, and also because of the lack of reliable information about him.

Now, De Lange has produced *Miyamoto Musashi: A Life in Arms*, a comprehensive story of the swordsman which draws on the aforementioned biographies but also assembles snippets of information from a vast array of other sources, many of which have been unearthed only recently by Japanese historians amid the ongoing revival of interest in Musashi's life. In writing this book, De Lange has used some 40 English texts and over 180 Japanese sources to paint the most complete picture of Musashi yet written in English. He also includes the full English translation of the *Kokura Hibun*, the epitaph erected by Musashi's adopted son Iori in 1654.

The book is filled with anecdotes about the exceptional warrior, drawn from these historical sources. One from the *Bukoden* describes Musashi's unusual strength, even as an old man in failing health. When asked how to select suitable lengths of bamboo to use as flag poles:

> *Musashi asked him to hand him a bunch and, holding them at their lower end with one hand, brandished them as one would a sword, causing several lengths to break under the strain … Master Yoriyuki laughed heartily and said, "Truly, that is a good way of selecting the right bamboo, but who on earth is able to brandish a bunch of bamboo with one hand like you?" (p. 113)*

We further learn about Musashi's pained relationship with his father Muni, himself a nationally renowned swordsman. Far from barely knowing his father, De Lange demonstrates that Musashi spent years at Muni's Kyushu dojo while a young man in his twenties. We also learn something about Musashi's desire to have children of his own: he adopted two sons, raised a short-lived daughter, and became a respected father figure to many of his own students. Unlike Yoshikawa's picture of Musashi as a wild-eyed ruffian, we get a sense of him as a complex man with both a deep sense of humility and a delicate sense of pride; a well-loved friend to many, but also something of a loner at heart. We feel the tension between Musashi's need for freedom and his longing to settle down.

Much of this is due to De Lange's vivid writing style, which is accessible and written almost like a novel. This is a strength of the work, as it makes this historical tale come vividly to life. However, it can sometimes be a source of mild frustration: De Lange takes pains to back up his findings with solid historical evidence (there are 45 pages of welcome notes) but at times he indulges in what seems like speculation about Musashi's state of mind and inner conflicts. One such example concerns Musashi's time as an advisor to Lord Hosokawa Tadatoshi in Kumamoto:

> *[Musashi] had come to cherish his independence, yet it was with a tinge of sadness that at times the old swordsman observed the self-important daily hustle and bustle on the castle grounds from the veranda of his yashiki. At such times he felt compelled to leave the protective yet strangely oppressive walls of Kumamoto castle to seek peace and quiet among nature. (p.112)*

De Lange then goes on to quote the *Bushu Denraiki* regarding Musashi's habit of going out of doors to pursue falconry. I found myself wondering about the basis for this insight into Musashi's emotional state—a letter, perhaps? An account from a student? Perhaps it was, in fact, just a bit of creative conjecture on De Lange's part.

In the end, however, I feel that if anyone is qualified to fill in the missing details of Musashi's life, it is De Lange, who has surely done more research on the subject than any other non-Japanese. De Lange's great achievement is in creating a work that walks the fine line between academic research and accessible writing. In doing so, he has painted a remarkably vibrant portrait of Musashi, one that reveals all the contradictions of a remarkable life full of triumphs and disappointments, thrilling victories as well as bitter losses. For all his astonishing, almost superhuman accomplishments, the lingering impression of Musashi is of someone endearingly flawed, and deeply human.

This book is unquestionably a must-read for any student of budo, and especially for those who have read De Lange's previous translations. *A Life in Arms* draws together the relevant information in a logical, readable fashion to form a cohesive portrait of a man who, perhaps now more than ever, should be viewed as one of the greatest martial artists who ever lived.

ARMING THE KIDS

by Tyler Rothmar

Chilean Kendo Federation President Miguel Ullivarri sat down with Kendo World to explain why children's bōgu is the missing ingredient for his country's kendo growth.

"I remember when I came to Japan, there were about 300 kendo practitioners in Chile, and that was ten years ago", says Miguel Ullivarri. "Now, a decade later, we still have about 300 people, and there are very few children involved. It's ageing, but it isn't growing."

Like many kendo nations around the world, Chile is starting to pay close attention to its demographics. While a wave of beginners led by too few sensei comes with its own set of pedagogical problems, the inverse scenario, an ageing cohort with no beginners to teach, puts the future of any federation at risk.

To avoid this, Chile is taking steps to bring more young people into the fold. It isn't easy, but the hope is that Chilean kendo will grow in strength as well as size.

Hurdles to clear

"I became president one year ago," says Ullivarri. "All our efforts have been concentrated on coming here [to Tokyo] for the 16th WKC, and usually our federation concentrates on international competitions. The development and teaching of kendo, according to Chilean law, belongs to the clubs. So we do have government support, but it's never enough."

Part of the challenge is geographical. Glance at a map and you'll see that, as countries go, Chile's shape is rather unique. It has more than 4,000km of longitudinal coastline, yet the average width along this considerable length is just 180km. Dojos are dotted more or less single file from north to south, and getting the national team together for training, much less trips abroad for competition, takes up much of the federation's budget, Ullivarri says.

The problem of how to get kids to take up the art is compounded by economic conditions. While there are programs in place to give kids a chance to try kendo, he says, anyone who gets serious "has to buy *bōgu*, *shinai*, *kendo-gi* and *hakama*, all of which come to no less than $700 USD in Chile."

Meanwhile, an individual earning the country's new minimum wage (as of July 1, 2015) will have just 241,000 Chilean Pesos, or $372 USD, at month's end.

Growing its kendo under such conditions isn't easy, but Chile is a country with a plan.

Strong kids, strong future

"What we need right now more than anything else is *bōgu* for kids," says Ullivarri.

Kaiken, his home club in the coastal city of Viña del Mar, near Santiago, came up with one solution several years back. Using money from the city's government, they bought *shinai* and paid an instructor to teach kendo in public schools for three months at a time. "The kids get a kendo experience, maybe the instructor brings them to the dojo from time to time, and a few will go on," he says of the early effort.

The next step was opening practice for children at the Kaiken dojo each Saturday, free of charge. A doctor donated five pairs of *kote*, someone else brought a few *shinai*, and the club began to collect pieces of *bōgu*. "We really wanted the kids to enjoy doing kendo. That was the driving force behind our efforts," Ullivarri says.

Meanwhile, a private dojo began offering children's classes for a fee, and last year, the growing Korean community opened a dojo for children under the direction of Jihoon Kwak.

In March, students from all three youth dojo came together for Chile's first kids *gasshuku* in Viña del Mar, organized by the Kaiken dojo. Ullivarri says it was a hit: "We're only 1.5 hours away from Santiago, and many of the parents got really excited and organized car pools. It was a very successful one-day experience."

Today, efforts to involve more young people in kendo are picking up pace. Ullivarri has met with a representative from the Ministry of Sport to plan a Kendo Formative School set to open in 2016, and later this year a seminar to train people who want to teach children will be held.

"Our plan is to take the model we have started and put it into the school system," he continues. "There are now 11 regular clubs, from Arica at the country's northern

tip, to Puerto Montt in the south. They span more than 3,000km. Our objective is to give each club the tools they need to teach kendo for free in the public schools around them.

"I feel that in Chile, this is the only way to really get children into kendo, given the expenses. So we will provide the instructor, the *shinai* and *bōgu*, and they can go to the schools and offer to provide an educational opportunity for free. We need only a regular block of time, and the gymnasium, and it will not cost anything for the school or the families of the kids, who can learn in an environment they're used to. The federation will pay the instructors on an hourly basis. This is our idea."

Ullivarri thinks kendo can complement the kinds of clubs typically found in Chilean schools such as football, tennis, and taekwondo. The missing ingredient, he says, is *bōgu*.

"We're looking for any federation, any club, anyone who can help. Of course we will arrange and pay for the shipping. We were very pleased to receive used adult *bōgu* from the All Japan Kendo Federation in 2008, but now we are focusing on the kids.

"We can concentrate on competition as much as we like, but if our people are starting kendo at 17 or 20 years old, it's difficult to have a real medal target. If they start at 7 or 8 years, then we can start to think about getting to the top level of kendo in competition. If we can increase the kendo population, we can get more support from the government, and the wheel will begin to turn. If we can teach in the schools, we will double our kendo population quickly. Not all kids who try it will go on, but maybe some will remember and come back to kendo later in life. The positive effect for the kendo community in Chile and in Latin America will be hard to measure."

To donate children's bōgu to the Chilean Kendo Federation or otherwise get in touch with them, please email kendochile@gmail.com

MARTIAL AIDS
THE SHOGUN TRAVELLER BAG™ BY SHOGUN KENDOGU

By Michael Ishimatsu-Prime

Kendo World is always keen to hear about new technologies and products that make the lives of kendoka safer and easier, and maybe even cheaper. In past issues of KW we have looked at new products such as the Carbon Shinai and the *tsuki* protector to name but a few. The clever bods at Shogun Kendogu debuted a new product at the 16th WKC—the Shogun Traveller Bag™—that is sure to be of interest to those who travel regularly on aeroplanes with their *bōgu*. KW Skyped Blake Bennett, director of international sales at Shogun Kendogu, to find out more about this product.

Kendo World: Blake, thank you for taking the time to talk with us today.

Blake Bennett: It's no problem.

KW: So, in a nutshell, what is the Shogun Traveller Bag™?

BB: Simply, it is a new type of *bōgu* bag that allows a kendoka to put both his or her *bōgu* and *shinai* in the same bag, together with some clothes.

KW: What was the reason for making it?

BB: Well, travelling with *bōgu* and *shinai* can be a challenge. As part of the trials and tribulations of calling oneself a kendoka, journeying abroad with *bōgu* in tow plagues those who fancy a bash beyond the regular training spot. I'm sure that we have all thought, as I have done, "I should've been a swimmer" as I cram my gear into the back of a car or taxi. But for those of us who require a plane to get to our destination, perhaps the most frequent inconvenience is the rigmarole and cost associated with checking in an extra bag, specifically, *shinai*.

KW: But doesn't *shinai* count as "sporting equipment"?

BB: Sometimes it does, and sometimes it doesn't. Many airlines notoriously change their policies on sporting equipment, extra baggage, and oversized baggage without warning. Yet no matter how much one pleads, flirts, or attempts to explain that it is "sporting equipment" and that the extra cost outweighs the price of the item itself, more often than not replies cite airline policy with smatterings of "too bad".

KW: When I first used to fly back to England from Japan with *bōgu* in tow, it was never a problem. The baggage allowance used to be any number of checked-in bags up

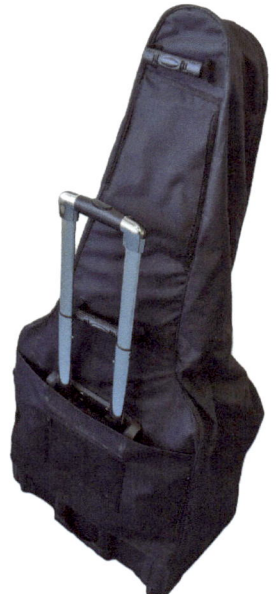

The Shogun Traveller Bag™   The Shogun Traveller Bag™ with the *shinai* section folded down

to a total of 23kg. I could have all my clothes, Christmas presents and other necessities in my rucksack. That together with my *shinai* bag totalled about 15kg. Then my *bōgu* would count as sporting equipment and have its own allowance.

BB: Exactly. That used to be the case, but then around 2010 or 2011, many airline companies changed the rules to one piece of checked-in baggage up to 23kg. That was apparently to "make the baggage policy easier to understand". That means that, if your *bōgu* was counted as sporting equipment, you would only have to pay for the cost of one bag—the *shinai* bag. But if they didn't recognise your *bōgu* as sports equipment you'd have to pay for two extra bags.

KW: I always embarked from Japan when flying with *bōgu*, so the check-in staff had always heard of kendo and accepted that it was sporting equipment. If the check-in staff in England questioned my *bōgu* bag when I was making my return to Japan, I could always say that it was fine on the way here.

BB: But for many people who fly to Japan or fly between

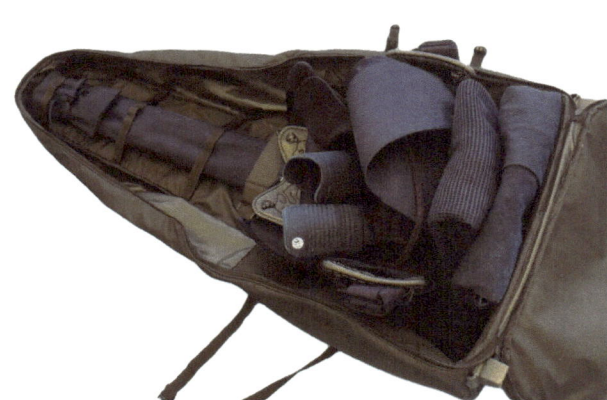

How to pack the Shogun Traveller Bag™

The Shogun Traveller Bag™ with *shinai* inside

different European countries, for example, that is often a problem as many check-in staff do not know kendo, and *bōgu* is not on their list of sporting equipment.

KW: When this baggage rule change was implemented, what did you do?

BB: I used to put everything in a surfboard bag which definitely counted as sporting equipment. It was long enough for *shinai*, and could hold *bōgu* and clothes, too. It wasn't ideal, but it had to do. Also, it wasn't really safe enough for my *dō*, which could have been easily crushed and broken.

Born of frustration from countless situations like what I have described, I started to think about designing a *bōgu* bag that could carry everything. Alex Bennett, my brother, also travels overseas with *bōgu* a lot, so I sought his advice and guidance on what the bag should be like.

KW: Can you describe the bag?

BB: The bag resembles an oversized guitar case. It is big enough to fit a set of *kendō-gi* and *hakama*, a set of *bōgu*, three *shinai* and still have room for clothes. It is also made from light but durable fabric and the weight of the bag alone is only 4kg (8.8lbs), allowing more freedom when travelling with the usual consignment required on a kendo-related trip. It has caster wheels so it can be transported like a regular suitcase, and the bag has handles at different positions so it can be carried easily. Most importantly, it allows kendo equipment to be carried together, or separately, depending on the costs associated with extra baggage or over-sized baggage.

Simply, if the airline insists on charging extra to check-in more than one item, the *shinai* can be inserted into the bag, and more than likely, the item will be classed as over-sized. Alternatively, if the airline charges more for over-sized baggage, the bag can roll down into the shape of a conventional *bōgu* bag, and the *shinai* can be checked-in separately as usual. Whatever costs an airline charges for either scenario, if at all, the Shogun Traveller Bag™ allows the traveller to select the cheapest option. In many cases, over-sized luggage is not charged to the passenger.

KW: How many different designs did you come up with before you settled on the final one? How long was that process?

BB: I have a spare room full of prototypes, each a bit better than the last but all based around the same basic design. The overall process took around one year in total.

KW: What problems did you have designing it?

BB: The biggest issue we faced was convincing manufacturers in Japan to make the bag in the first place. People simply just didn't see a need for it. I guess that's the nature of living in a country where you don't need to travel too far for kendo. When you do, the bullet train makes life easy. Once we found a manufacturer that shared our vision, we were away laughing.

KW: How has the Shogun Traveller Bag™ been received so far?

BB: We had a great deal of interest at the WKC and took many orders. Because of its popular demand, there is currently a short wait on orders for it. The bag itself retails at US$249, including international postage, but all orders entitle the customer to a US$100 discount off any full set of *bōgu* listed on the Shogun Kendogu web store. You can make an order at www.ShogunKendogu.com in the "Shinai & Bōgu Bags" category.

KW: Best of luck with this product and thank you for taking the time to talk to us today.

BB: Thank you for the opportunity.

Kenneth Reed being observed by Mori Takashi Sokan Sōshō at the sadō seminar

Tea and the Kenshi

Sadō, the Way of Tea, and Kendo, the Way of the Sword.

By Kenneth Reed

I believe that no martial art symbolises the spirit of the warrior more than kendo. Although the steel of the katana has been replaced by the bamboo and leather of the *shinai*, all other aspects of the samurai spirit live on in the practice of kendo.

Kendo requires a strong spirit, physical strength, and an enduring mental attitude to avoid defeat. To strike a "killing" blow, good technique is required, but victory also requires a single-mindedness to defeat one's opponent. With time, many kenshi come to realise that the true opponent they must defeat is themselves. Attaining the state of *mushin* (empty mind) is the place that all kenshi try to reach. This is why the study of kendo is a lifetime pursuit, and that it is a journey more than a destination.

> "A warrior has no confusion in his mind...this is true emptiness"
>
> Miyamoto Musashi

My first trip to Japan was to attend the 2011 Kitamoto Foreign Kendo Leader's Seminar. During one portion of the seminar, K8-dan Hayashi Tatsuo-sensei told the participants, "We are not just teaching you a martial art, we are introducing you to our culture. Kendo is the embodiment of Japanese culture." I was touched by this thought and the words of Hayashi-sensei. However, I have come to believe that there is another "Way" that is just as much the embodiment of Japanese culture as kendo: *sadō*, the Way of Tea.

The Japanese tea ceremony is also often called "*cha-noyu*", or "*chadō*", but the name that we use in the Omote Senke school is "*sadō*". *Sadō* is a highly choreographed ritual of preparing and serving Japanese green tea, called *matcha*, along with traditional Japanese sweets to balance the strong bitter taste of the tea. The process for making the tea and serving it within proper expectations is called *temae*. Preparing tea in this ceremony means pouring all of one's attention or focus into the predefined movements of the ceremony. In time one comes to realise the whole process is not even about drinking the tea, but is about the aesthetics, the preparing of a bowl of tea from one's heart, and the effort to make a beautiful cup of tea for the guest. The host of the ceremony must always consider the guest with every movement and gesture. The selection and placement of the tea utensils is considered from the viewpoint of the guest. Even the selection of the sentiment written on the hanging scroll is chosen with the guest in mind. On the evening before my last kendo grading, my sensei chose a kanji, which was loosely translated as "Keep calm, drink tea." I thought of this prior to taking my exam, as a way of focusing my mind and actions.

The *sadō* concept of pouring all of one's attention or focus into the predefined movements of the tea ceremony is my first place of comparison between *sadō* and kendo. Both disciplines have this state of mind and focus as a goal. The older sensei that I have encountered in kendo, especially those that I met in Japan, have tried to instil a similar understanding when it comes to kendo. Kendo, in its purest and non-tournament sense, is not about defeating the opponent. It is about doing your best, and performing your most beautiful kendo. I can remember, when standing in line waiting for my chance to do *keiko* with a high-ranking sensei, my determination to score an *ippon* off him. Of course, that was exactly the wrong focus. My focus should have been much like that of the tea host, showing my kendo to him from my heart. Demonstrating my effort to execute the most beautiful kendo strike possible should be my goal; or put in *sadō* terms, my gift to him. If that is done properly, the scoring of an *ippon* has little or no meaning. Performing beautiful kendo is the goal and the gift. I did not understand this before I began studying *sadō*, and it helped me to better understand this aspect of kendo.

There is an old Japanese story that in my research I have read numerous times and in many variations, but the crux of the story is as follows:

> *A master of sadō (the Way of the tea ceremony), was challenged to a duel by a rōnin who was confident of winning with ease. Since he could not refuse the challenge without loss of honour, the tea master prepared to die. He went to call on a neighbouring master of kenjutsu and asked him to teach him how to die properly. 'Your intention is most laudable. You are unique. Most students come ask me how to use a sword. You come to me asking how to die. Before I teach you the art of dying, please serve me a cup of tea,' said the kenjutsu master, 'and I should be very happy to help you, but first of all kindly serve me a cup of tea please.'*

> *The tea master was delighted to have the chance to practise his skill, probably for the last time. Forgetting about his impending catastrophe, the tea master prepared tea in the manner as he always did—as if there were nothing else in the world that mattered except for serving the tea. Deeply moved by the tea master's intense, but natural concentration, the sword master exclaimed, 'That's it! Your state of mind when you perform the tea ceremony is all that is required. First think of serving tea to an honoured guest and act accordingly. Take off your coat, fold it carefully and place your fan on top of it, exactly as you have just done. Then draw your katana and raise it above your head, ready to strike when the opponent attacks, and concentrate on this action alone. Draw your sword and close your eyes. When you hear his kiai, strike him with your sword. The contest will probably end with a mutual slaying."*

> *The next morning when he went to meet the rōnin, he followed the sword master's advice to the letter. The tea master boldly stood before his opponent, the embodiment of concentration. Cowed with fear inspired by the superior concentration of his adversary, the rōnin who had previously seen a coward, now faced the personification of bravery. Instead of advancing to attack, the rōnin threw down his own katana and prostrating himself before the tea master, humbly asked forgiveness for his unspeakable conduct.*

On the surface this traditional story from Japan is about how a master of tea overcame a samurai warrior who challenged him to a duel. But it also shows how if you are the master of yourself, you can be the master of anything. To me it also shows the closeness in concept between kendo and *sadō*.

I myself came to study *sadō* after failing in my first attempt at achieving 4-dan in kendo. After I failed to pass the examination, and after an appropriate time of self-pity, I put on my *bōgu*, picked up my *shinai*, and began to train anew. One night after *keiko*, I spoke with one of the sensei who was also one of my examiners. He told me that my problem was not the mechanics of my kendo, but my lack of focus. He pointed out that I spent too much time thinking about the last point, too much time concentrating on the next point, and not enough focus on allowing the beauty of my kendo to show.

I was determined to address this failing so I contacted the wife of my kendo sensei. She has been a practitioner of *sadō* for years, and I asked her if I could attend lessons with her. I knew from watching her serve tea once before that the development of focus and calm seemed to be two of the more obvious results of the study of *sadō*. Just ask any modern kenshi that has attempted to sit in *seiza* for anything more than five minutes to appreciate the effort needed in sitting in such a manner—in *sadō*, *seiza* can last much longer than five minutes. Getting your mind past the pain and numbness in your legs alone can be a Herculean effort. A few weeks later I began a journey that has resulted in the *chasaku* (tea scoop) becoming as much a part of my kendo life as the *shinai*.

I met my tea sensei, Takako Hori, on a Saturday afternoon. The class was conducted at a local Buddhist temple in Southern California. Since I was to be her newest student by a few years, I could not attend the class with the other students until I learned the basics of *sadō*. My lesson began in the *mizuya*, or water room, not the tearoom. Put in Western terms, my tea lessons began in the kitchen, washing dishes.

My sensei first taught me how to clean the tea bowl, and the other utensils. It was on this first day that she also taught me the folding of the *chakin*, a small rectangular white linen or hemp cloth mainly used to wipe the tea bowl between successive servings of the guests. My sensei explained this to me and then demonstrated the preparation and placement of the *chakin*. I would later learn that like all aspects of serving tea, this is to be done with marked precision. The *chakin* is taken from a flat water bowl, the water is wrung from the cloth in a manner called "*chakin-shibori*" (the English translation is "*chakin* wringing"), it is then precisely folded and placed inside the tea bowl. The left hand (bottom hand) turns counter clockwise, and the right hand (top hand) turns clockwise.

This motion of wringing the *chakin* is the same as the ideal action for gripping the *shinai* in kendo. Because the phrase is Japanese, it is not often used here in the West, but during our annual kendo seminar at a dojo that I often attend, the 8-dan sensei from Japan used this very phase when discussing and demonstrating the feel and grip that should be kept in mind when holding the *shinai*.

During this year's annual *sadō* seminar, two years after I began my first lesson, I was to perform the part of the demonstration that involved the serving of *usucha* (thin tea). This was to be my first time serving tea in front of anyone other than my sensei and fellow students. Many of the members of my *dōmenkai* were to be in attendance, along with the Sōshō (tea master) from Japan. Normally the person performing the demonstration serves the tea to the guests and the Sōshō makes corrections to his form or posture from his position of observation at the front of the dais. In my case, because of the language barrier, the Sōshō moved to sit right beside me with my *sadō* sensei acting as an interpreter. I was very nervous, but in time I settled into the rhythm of performing the *temae*. The Sōshō was kind and understanding.

I suspect that prior to the demonstration, the Sōshō had been informed that I did not understand Japanese, but that I am a student of kendo. During the demonstration the Sōshō enlightened me to the fact that not only the *chakin-shibori*, but also the actual holding of the *chashaku* are kendo related, or have *kenjutsu* origins. When holding the *chashaku* in the right hand, it is to be held much in the same manner that the kenshi holds the *shinai*, and that he should hold the *shinai* not much firmer than when dipping the *chashaku* into the *kama* (the hot water kettle) to make the tea.

The Sōshō also made clear to me that when serving tea, though the server must focus on each task at hand, he must also "feel" the needs of the guest. He must overcome the pain in his legs (sitting in *seiza* for extended periods may be the reason why few people undertake the study of *sadō* these days), concentrate on his breathing and focus on giving his heart to the serving of tea. This is the Way of Tea. But this is also the Way of the Sword. As if to remind me of this fact, the Sōshō, himself a kendoka, told me, "Kenny-san, it is much like *sen-no-sen* in kendo; you must feel your guest." He said this with a knowing smile.

Historically, *sadō* was conducted only by men, primarily by monks and *bushi*, so it is no surprise that the samurai would interchange *sadō* and *kenjutsu* actions in their practice of the two disciplines. However, like most Westerners, I had thought serving tea was done by women wearing beautiful kimonos; little did I know that kendo and *sadō* are perhaps one and the same.

As I have come to understand them, both kendo and *sadō* put little emphasis on the intellectual explanations of their respective disciplines; the experience of learning is more important. Masters of both arts do not simply lecture on self-control, they show their students its importance. At the *sadō* seminar that I spoke of earlier, the Sōshō told us not to simply ask the master questions; the Way of Tea is a life journey and you will learn by doing. My own kendo sensei, Taro Ariga, has often given me a similar response when a question about kendo has come to my mind, and in the way of modern communication, I simply sent a quick email with my question. His response was, "Kenny-san, I can't teach you kendo by email, come to the dojo, we will discuss it during and after *keiko*." Again, the two Ways may really be one.

In *sadō*, Sen no Rikkyū, the founder of the modern Japanese tea ceremony, stressed the importance of this kind of calm, concentrated mind during the *temae*. Rikkyū was also the first to emphasise several key aspects of the tea ceremony, including rustic simplicity, directness of approach, and honesty of self. Rikkyū was heavily responsible for working *wabi-sabi* (finding beauty in the very simple, imperfect, impermanent, and incomplete) into the Japanese tea ceremony. I will confess that this term "*wabi-sabi*" is still difficult for me, and my understanding of the concept itself is still evolving.

I understand that *wabi-sabi* has no direct translation in the English language. However, even with my limited understanding of the concept, I do know that simplicity, directness, and honesty of self are also key aspects of kendo. The concept of *wabi-sabi* is often extended to include the beauty of impermanence. A common example is *sakura* (cherry blossom). The Japanese believe that cherry blossoms are more beautiful because they do not last forever. There is great beauty in the impermanence of an action, and treating each moment as the most important moment in life is a goal which Rikkyū emphasised in the practice of *sadō*, teaching that each step in serving has a beauty of its own. This is also found in kendo when executing a men strike the best that you can possibly do, irrespective of the presence of an opponent, observers, or even the desire to win. I think this may be the *wabi-sabi* of kendo.

One of Rikkyū's most famous teachings is, "A person must discard all embarrassment when training in tea: this is the foundation of its mastery". Since my understanding of the Japanese language has not progressed beyond a few words and phrases, I am not sure if there is a similar maxim for training in kendo. However, as I have come to understand it, one of the goals of a kenshi in his quest to perfect his fighting technique is to perfect himself, improving day-by-day and weeding out personal inadequacies, together with developing humility, courtesy, awareness, and largeness of spirit. The words are different but the road to mastery appears to me to be the same.

At its core kendo can help develop posture, poise, grace under pressure, clarity of thought, and the power of concentration. The effort to attain a calm state is an effort to discard all that is outside the dojo while inside the dojo.

In *sadō*, I recently learned the Japanese phrase "*ichigo ichie*". Its meaning, as I have come to understand it, means to live consciously in each present moment. Rather than worrying about future uncertainties, continue the process of watching where you are and then move forward a step at a time, as though that step is all that there is to life. By moving in this way, tomorrow takes care of itself, and builds itself. Of course *ichigo ichie* must also be a major tenet of kendo. How many times have I heard my sensei say "Don't stop, …go through"? This common admonishment is to caution students who become careless or frequently stop techniques midway to "try again", rather than moving on with the technique despite the mistake. In a life-or-death struggle, there is no chance to "try again".

*Sōshō and participants of the sadō seminar
(L to R: Takako Hori, Kenneth Reed, Mori Takashi Sokan Sōshō, Ayako Ariga and Mamoru Takashina)*

As I stated at the beginning of this article, the study of kendo is a life journey. I have come to believe that we all are on the journey. Sometimes we take a short break, sometimes a longer rest, but maybe the journey itself is the prize even more than reaching the destination. For me, *sadō* has helped in that journey. Though I must confess, at this point I am not sure whether *sadō* has helped my kendo, or if kendo has helped my understanding of *sadō*. Perhaps they are both intertwined in my life's journey. I stumble and come up short of my goals on a daily basis, but kendo and *sadō* always have my back, and are always there as a welcome well of support when needed. I hold the *chashaku* as I would hold the *shinai*, I keep my back straight imagining that I am in *chūdan-no-kamae*. I practise *sadō* in my mind before beginning a kendo match (my sensei calls this "air *sadō*") as it calms my mind and puts me in a harmonious place.

When I am not swinging the *shinai* or holding the *chashaku*, I am a practising criminal defence attorney in Southern California. I have daily battles with prosecutors and judges, and both kendo and *sadō* are welcome respites. My mental and physical well-being have benefited from the practice of both kendo and *sadō*. The Way of the Sword and the Way of Tea have both helped me to improve my skills and begin understanding of the "Way of the Lawyer".

I cannot promise that everybody will enjoy the study of *sadō* as much as I have done in these last two years, nor can I promise that it will be instrumental in passing the next kendo promotion examination, as it was for me when I passed 4-dan. However, what I can promise is that merging the concepts of kendo and *sadō* will not be wasted effort in one's journey along the way.

BOOK REVIEW

CHINESE MARTIAL ARTS
from Antiquity to the Twenty-First Century

By Peter A. Lorge
Review by Yulin Zhuang

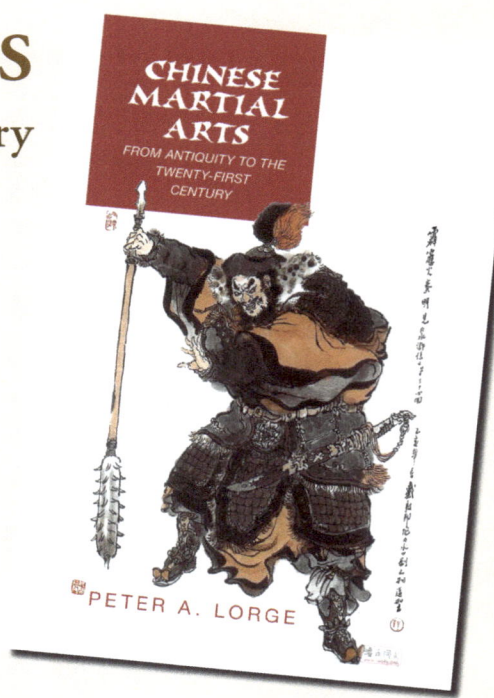

*Chinese Martial Arts
from Antiquity to the Twenty-First Century*
Peter A. Lorge
Cambridge University Press
ISBN: 9780521878814
282 pages

Oftentimes, the oral history of a martial art can be its own worst enemy. Legends get passed down as fact, changing or being embellished as time passes. None of us wants to call our teachers liars, but many times what they believe about the origins of what they teach is simply wrong. While there has been a great deal of excellent Chinese language scholarship on the issue, much of this has not filtered through into the popular understanding.

Chinese martial arts are as rife with exaggeration or legends as any other. Unlike in Japan, where martial arts were practised by the elite, and lineages and students meticulously recorded, much of the history of the Chinese martial arts has been in the hands of the ordinary folk, as something to turn to in times of trouble. While martial arts were practised by elites in ancient Chinese history, by the time of the Song Dynasty (960-1279) and later, the references in classical texts to military training (especially archery) were viewed as purely allegorical rather than practical.

The stewards of Chinese martial arts have, for the past few centuries, been the peasants. There is an old saying in China—"Heaven is high and the Emperor is far away." For much of Chinese history, villagers have had to rely on their own martial skills to defend themselves against bandits, rebellions, or foreign invasions. However, this is not representative of Chinese history as a whole. In Confucius' day, archery skills were considered essential for the educated nobility. However, as time passed, the Chinese literati began to denigrate military skill and subordinate it to intellectual skills. Unlike in Japan, where the elite literati practised and made numerous records, In China the martial arts traditions passed into the peasantry, where illiteracy and oral tradition were the norm.

In *Chinese Martial Arts from Antiquity to the Twenty-First Century*, Peter A. Lorge takes the long view and a trained historian's rigour to the textual history of martial arts in China. Relying on contemporary accounts, he builds an in-depth picture of martial arts in China from the earliest accounts to the modern era. The book also examines in depth what we know about the true origins of many popular Chinese martial arts, such as tai-chi and Shaolin kung-fu, and punctures many of the myths surrounding them. Does the vaunted 1500 year history of Shaolin kung-fu sound a little bit too good to be true? After a reference to the Shaolin temple sending a cadre of warrior monks to help the future Emperor Tang Taizu (598-649), no one else visiting the Shaolin temple for the next 900 years mentions any martial artists in connection with the temple until the 16th century. Even then, after a series of defeats, a visitor looking for Shaolin's famed martial arts in 1679 found only a few starving monks and no martial arts. There were martial artists present during the Qing Dynasty (1644-1912) but the reputation far outstripped the reality. In fact, the rebuilding of Shaolin can be traced to the wildly successful movie *Shaolin Temple* (1982), whose on-site filming found the temple run down and defunct of both religious or martial arts activity. While this is not news to scholars of Chinese martial arts, Lorge does an excellent job of placing the Shaolin tradition in the larger context of Chinese martial arts in general.

The book also delves into the subject of women warriors, a topic often overlooked. Lorge traces the long tradition of female fighters from Fu Hao (circa. 1200 BC) in the Shang Dynasty to the story of Mulan. There have been many celebrated female fighters in Chinese history. Women were not confined to the home, but took an active role in protecting themselves and their community. For long periods, China was ruled by foreigners from the steppe, whose martial tradition included women warriors. *Chinese Martial Arts from Antiquity to the Twenty-First Century* devotes significant space to the topic of women in martial arts throughout Chinese history.

For large parts of history, we do not have much reference to specific techniques or schools, and the book tends to become a simple history of soldiers and military organisations. Lorge avoids the sensational and focuses as much as possible on the broader martial arts and military communities across various dynasties, and tracks the changes in perception towards martial arts. He devotes space not just to the bloody bits of military history, but also to martial arts as a performance and its oft-exaggerated connection to religious practice.

Lorge tends to confine himself to verifiable historical fact, which does mean that he shies away from any controversial statements. The much-debated origins of tai-chi, xingyi, and bagua get a mere three pages, which consist mainly of noting that the scholarly evidence does not back up many of the claims of practitioners. Nevertheless, he shows a refreshing lack of bias in his approach to the topic, which helps lend gravitas to his work.

Of particular interest to students of Japanese martial arts are the changes to Chinese military tactics that evolved out of raids by Japanese pirates. In the middle of the Ming Dynasty, raids by so-called "Japanese Pirates" or "*wokou*", were the scourge of the coastal regions. The current controversy among historians about how "Japanese" the pirates truly were is ignored in favour of describing the evolution of Chinese military tactics. Lorge notes the initial superiority of Japanese swordsmanship to Chinese swordsmanship, although he insists on calling it "Japanese fencing"; a jarring use of flawed terminology. Nevertheless, the use of spears and polearm weapons and better training manuals were ultimately able to overcome the *wokou* raids.

The illustrations in the book were somewhat disappointing. While he includes photographs of very early Chinese weaponry in the first few chapters, the rest of the book's illustrations consisted entirely of line sketches of operatic characters drawn at the end of the 19th century whose historical accuracy is dubious at best. More effort to obtain contemporary portrayals of martial arts or photographs of historical weapons for the middle two thousand years of Chinese history would have strengthened the book.

In the end, however, my main criticism of the book is simply that it left me wanting more. This book is a magisterial effort and a must-read for any serious scholar of martial arts. One can only hope that Lorge will continue his research and produce more in-depth work in the future.

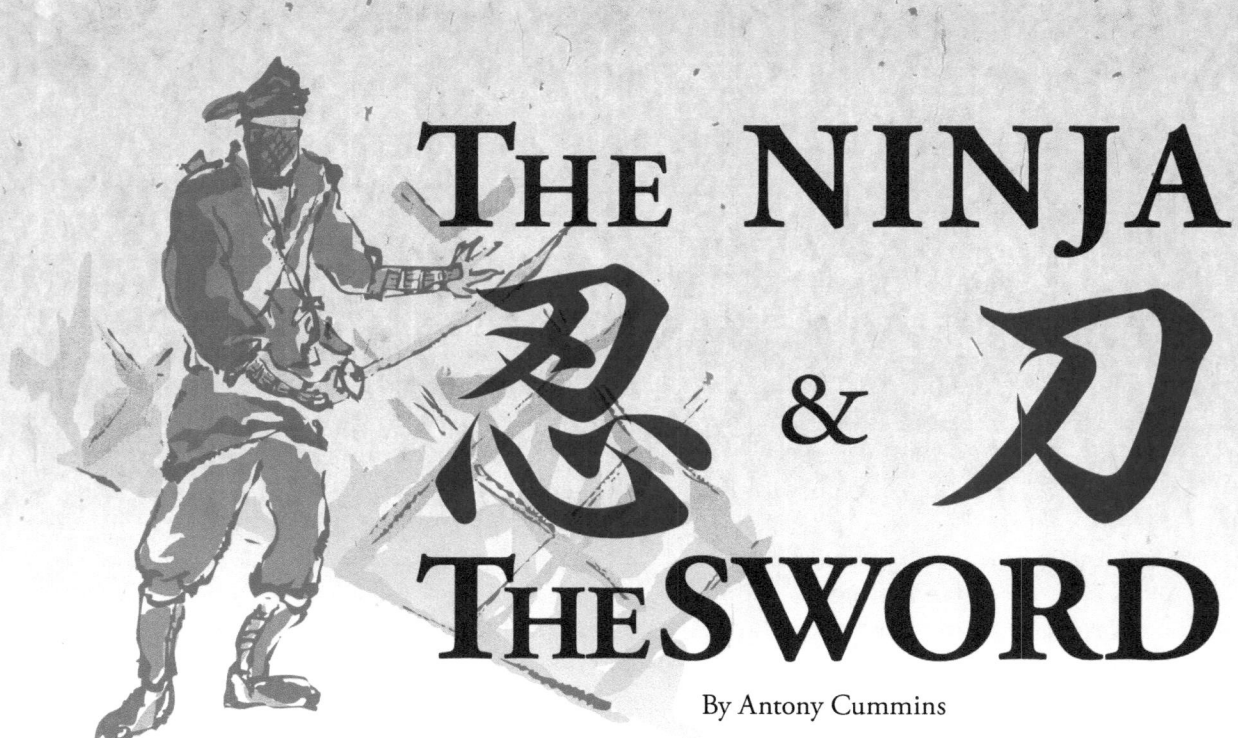

The Ninja & The Sword

By Antony Cummins

The popular image of the ninja is littered with misnomers and mistakes that are taken as pure fact when the reality is actually quite different. The most common error is that ninja are thought to have been in opposition to the samurai, when it was quite the reverse. The art of the ninja is known as *ninjutsu,* or more correctly as *shinobi no jutsu*—literally, *shinobi* (stealth) skills. These arts were used by the samurai to complement their normal training so that they could specialise in clandestine warfare and espionage—dispelling the peasant ninja versus the samurai myth. Also, the idea that there is a specific hand-to-hand system of fighting called "*ninpō taijutsu*" or the unarmed combat methods of the ninja is also a modern invention—a business package used to sell *jūjutsu* to a gullible Western audience. Which leads us to the other very popular myth—the ninja sword.

The *ninja-tō* 忍者刀 or *shinobi-gatana* (*katana*) 忍刀 is mistakenly considered by many to be a sword exclusively used by the ninja, and to be lesser in quality to the samurai blade. There are a few issues that this idea raises: first, the terms do not appear anywhere in historical sources, and have yet to be found in any manual. Second, in the warring periods when *shinobi no jutsu* was created, anyone from the lowest peasant to the shogun could carry swords, and it was only with the famous "sword hunts" in the late 1500s, and the Tokugawa period of peace that restrictions on weapons were enforced. Therefore, the idea of a ninja peasant with his inferior crafted sword runs against historical trends. He could have just inserted a normal sword at his waist as was the norm in Japan at the time. Nevertheless, the story is not so simple, and the myth of the ninja sword is a grey area.

The following selection of points will construct a basic outline of what is known about the sword and its use by the ninja (correctly known as *shinobi*), and will establish what is real, what is possible, and what is simply not true.

Modern Impressions of the 'Ninja Sword'

The following points make up the modern idea of what a ninja sword is, or should be. While they may not be wholly incorrect, they cannot be taken at face value.

The Square Tsuba

The iconic ninja item is the square hand guard, the tell-tale sign which automatically screams "ninja sword". However, it was not uncommon for sword guards to be square, and it was perfectly acceptable for any samurai or foot soldier to use a square *tsuba*. To date, there is not a single reference to *shinobi* exclusively using a square hand guard on their sword.

The Straight Blade

Alongside the square hand guard, the straight sword blade is another iconic point. Originally, straight swords came from China but were phased out as the Japanese sword evolved from around the tenth century. Straight bladed swords were still made as ceremonial objects, and some *katana* were almost straight, that is, with a minor curve of a few millimetres or less. In addition, some older and unused

The Ninja & The Sword
忍 & 刀

blades were shortened at the ends, which made them look straight. Spear and halberd blades were also cut down and mounted on sword handles for use by the lower ranked soldiers. Therefore, although not created straight, blades that looked straight did exist. Notwithstanding, I cannot find a connection between straight swords and ninja.

A Longer Scabbard for a Shorter Blade
In the mid-twentieth century, popular Japanese authors promoted the idea that a ninja sword had a shorter blade and a longer scabbard. The aim of this was to surprise the opponent with a faster draw. No identifiable source has been found to support this idea. At the same time, the notion of a removable tip on the scabbard was introduced, but the origin is unknown, and it must be considered fiction or an extension of the idea of a breathing hole (discussed below).

Historically Identifiable Attributes Given to the Swords Used by Ninja
Having identified the myths and common ideas related to ninja swords, the following are verifiable parts and descriptions.

Longer Sageo
The *sageo* (cord), found on a *shinobi*'s sword was generally longer than normal. The reason was that it was used for various skills such as "The seven cord arts" (rope tying) which appear in both the *Bansenshukai* and the *Natori-ryū Gunpō* military manuals.

Leather Tsuba
In the oral traditions of the Tenshin Shōden Katori Shintō-ryū sword school based in Chiba, there is a tradition that *shinobi* used a leather bound sword *tsuba* to stop it rattling.

Black Ink
The *Shōninki* manual (published as *True Path of the Ninja*) contains a difficult passage. It states that a *shinobi* should rub ink on his "body"; however, the ideogram here can mean "body of a human" or "body of a sword" (blade). It is highly probable that *shinobi* inked their swords to stop them reflecting in the light.

Breathing Hole
Two manuals—the *Shōninki* and the *Mizukagami*—both state that a *shinobi* can put a hole in the end of his scabbard and use it as a breathing tube while underwater.

Magical Symbols

To date, I have found only one ninja manual which claims that magical text should be written on the blade of a sword, but no reason is given. It was most likely to give power to its cutting ability, or to render it silent.

Smaller Tsuba

One intriguing yet obscure reference to a style of sword concerns the "*shinobi-zashi*" or "*shinobi* sidearm" which is described as having a *tsuba* which is smaller than average, and that this weapon was "used to decapitate people."

Historically Identifiable "Sword Skills"

The following skills or elements which appear in historical records.

Climbing Over a Wall

A *shinobi* would tie the *sageo* to his feet or to his *obi* belt. Next, he would place the sword handle upwards against a wall. Using the *tsuba* as a foot rest, the sword served as a step ladder as he reached upwards to take hold of the lip of the wall. After reaching the top, the longer than normal *sageo* tied to his foot was used to pull the sword up.

Breathing through the Scabbard

There are two methods given for this. The first was when diving in deep water, the *shinobi* came close to the surface and breathed through the tube. Alternatively, he could drive his sword into the riverbed, hook his feet under the *tsuba*, and then allow the scabbard to come out of the water so that he could breathe and hide. An interesting note is that the manuals indirectly associate the *wakizashi* short sword with this skill, most likely because it is too hard to breathe through a tube the length of a *katana* scabbard.

Searching a Dark Room

One of the more famous *shinobi* skills has a number of variations. The basic idea was to draw the sword out of the scabbard, but leave the tip just a few inches inside. Then, by holding the sword out in front with the scabbard resting on the edge, the length of the blade is doubled. This balancing act of scabbard on the blade was supported by the agent holding the *sageo* in his other hand, or attaching it to his belt. With this improvised probe, the *shinobi* (or person looking for a *shinobi*) would search the room by touching in the dark; and when they hit or tapped a person, they would immediately discard the scabbard and cut the adversary down.

Chasing an Enemy

A *shinobi* chasing an enemy would change the side of approach depending on what weapon he was carrying. If carrying a spear, he would approach from behind on the right. This would enable him to stab to his left—which is easier than stabbing to the right. However, if chasing with sword in hand, he approached from behind to the left. It is more difficult to cut across to the left if he is positioned on the right.

Walking through Doors

The *Bansenshukai* ninja manual states:

> "If the enemy has no room on their left, then hold the sword overhead. If there blockage is on the right side, then take *chūdan* or the middle guard with the intent to thrust."

After identifying an enemy on the inside of a doorway, the *shinobi* knew how he would be attacked, and how to counterattack.

Conclusion

Taking all of the above into consideration, the term "*shinobi-gatana*" or "ninja sword" is not historically accurate. Rather, it is better to take the stance of "sword used by a *shinobi*". An identifiable or unique kind of sword used by ninja does not appear in historical records. They are the adaptations used by the *shinobi*; and the manner in which they used the sword which made it unique, or at least separate from basic uses by samurai and foot-soldiers not trained in the art of *shinobi no jutsu*. Thus, a *shinobi* trained samurai or foot-soldier would use his sword to climb walls, find people in the dark, tie people up with the *sageo*, build shelters, even breathe underwater, or silence it for stealth in the night.

About the author: Antony Cummins is an author and TV co-host who specialises in redefining the history of the ninja and is the founder of the Historical Ninjutsu Research Team. Together they have translated and published multiple ninjutsu manuals in English. If you are interested in the ninja, please visit Antony's website for information, photos and free downloads. Also, see Antony's new book Samurai and Ninja *(Tuttle, 2015) – out now in all good bookshops and online. www.natori.co.uk*

Shinai Sagas

Once Upon a Time in Japantown

By Charlie Kondek

In the rhythm of the Chinese restaurant, in the ritual of greeting, feeding and cleaning, in the patter of the owners' hard, glottal Chinese and the watery cascade of the Mexican cooks' Spanish, it was sometimes easy for Fugitive to forget he was in a self-imposed hell, that his presence here was an elongated act of penance to a God whose rules he'd invented. Carrying the plastic tubs from the tables to the kitchen, pushing the carts laden with trays of fresh glasses, plates and silverware to the two server stations, he'd become a familiar sight to the workers and the customers. A deceptively slight old man, a raven's wing fell from the crown of his head over eyes deeply lined like the pockets of his face, sad eyes, sad mouth, worn out from the effort of rueful smiling, a ghost in baggy corduroy pants, sports shirt and thin cardigan sweater beneath a plastic apron: Fujita—or "Fugitive", as he was known to himself by this English word he used as a kind of secret name.

The restaurant was not large, but it was wide, and occupied the ground floor of a building not entirely used, at an intersection in the Asian quarter where the sunlight and the lamplight slipped liquidly around corners and up the crooked street, and never got as high as the paper lanterns or the hand-lettered and neon signs advertising vegetables, liquor and phone cards. It was right where Chinatown touched the border of Japantown and overlapped Vietnamtown, Koreatown and Thaitown, and could have been any street in any town, the side of town hiding from the traffic and the sky. Fugitive was part of the frantic action of the place, the chatting Chinese boys and girls that waited on tables beneath the watchful eye of the matriarch behind the bar, the river-babble of customers and the soft Chinese love songs on the stereo system, the hot kitchen where the Mexican men, under the supervision of the patriarch, cooked in giant woks and boiling vats of oil to the sound of mariachi music and Texas croon. When the long chaos of a busy day was over, Fugitive would take out the last of the trash bags and linger in the alley letting the night air draw the sweat and soap from his face. He would smoke a cigarette and put off finishing work and going back to his room in Japantown, where he would sit by the window overlooking the eaves of the covered mall and try to drink himself gently into a sleep that evaded him and dreams which troubled him.

It was one night during a cigarette break in the middle of a week-night's shift that Fugitive first saw the girl with the pink hair. Two things surprised him. First,

Once Upon a Time in Japantown

that she, an American girl of high school or college age with outrageous pink hair, had walked straight out of a Japanese street scene with kendo equipment over her shoulder, wearing *keiko-gi* and *hakama*; the second were the tears streaming down the girl's face. She rushed down the alley, walking at a fast pace, didn't notice Fugitive, kept her gaze down and, though she wept abundantly, appeared to be holding back sobs. In an instant she was gone. That was a Tuesday. Fugitive cast his cigarette into an oily puddle and tried to put the strange sight out of his mind.

But something, curiosity or random chance or old instincts, caused him to stand in the same place at the same time the following Tuesday. He did not see her. But he saw her again on Thursday, and this time only for an instant as he hurled trash into the bin, her face lit by a neon sign that caused the tears on her face to glisten brightly and her strange, pink hair to glow like incandescent fire. She moved quickly in her grief and was once more gone.

Letting the screen door bang shut behind him as he re-entered the restaurant, Fujita shuffled thoughtfully into the kitchen, his thoughts on the girl, such a strange sight, like something out of a play. Sometimes, Fugitive was left to lock the restaurant up. He'd work, and he'd slip cash to pay for whiskey under a paperweight, and sit at the bar that he polished absently with a cloth while he lingered over the drink and let a cigarette whisper in the ashtray. All the lights except one would be off in the place, and in the blue glow of the aquarium the thin tendril of smoke would rise from the ashtray, a twisting thread pulled heavenward. In the long shadow behind the bar a towering statue of Guan Yin rose, as if growing out of the bottles of liquor on the shelves, its sightless eyes taking Fujita in, the folds of its robes concealing something he sought there. He sucked whiskey through the ice and pulled the cigarette to his lips. A finger of ash fell from the dead filter.

The next time he saw the girl he spoke to her. "Pardon me", he said, stepping from his place in the doorway, loud enough to be heard but not direct enough to startle. "I notice you practise kendo."

"Yes", she said, wiping tears from her cheeks with the butt of her palm as she turned to acknowledge him. She pulled herself together quickly and said politely, gesturing with one hand, "The dojo is near here and this is how I get back to where I parked. Do you, um. Do you practise kendo?"

"Yes", he said. "A long time ago. What is the name of the dojo?" She told him. He had an approximate idea of where it was in Japantown. "How long have you been practising kendo?"

"Not long," she said. "I'm not very good."

"I don't believe it. What would make an American girl want to practise kendo?"

"I keep asking myself that", she mumbled, thinking he wouldn't hear her. "I study Japanese language", she added more declaratively. "I like Japanese culture."

"You want to go to Japan?" She said she did. "I'm Japanese. But", he added quickly, "I live here now. Tell me more about your dojo."

They talked a while longer, about kendo, the conversation awkward for Fugitive as he tried to manoeuvre in a second language toward the things he wanted to say. To her, the conversation was an exercise in politeness: tell the old Japanese man about the dojo, invite him to join, show him how serious you are about kendo.

Fugitive's courage began to fail him. Some instinct made him bow deeply and say, "Please excuse me. It's not my business. But, you always seem sad when you come from kendo. Is it hard?"

She laughed, the laugh of one suddenly exposed, smiled politely and tried to explain quickly, "Yes, it's hard. But, it's making me stronger. So, one day I'll be okay."

Still bowing, Fujita said, "Kendo can be very difficult. It's okay to cry."

She nodded, half bowed. "I'm just not used to it. And, there aren't many women. And, I'm really not any good."

"Just need more practice," he said. Now he risked a glance in her direction. "Please, don't give up."

They saw each other often after that, and always in the same way, passing through the alley. It became easier over time for them to talk. He'd ask, sometimes in Japanese, "How was practice?" She'd answer, in fluent, halting, student Japanese. They talked about what she had practised, what drills and techniques, and sometimes he offered small pieces of advice, usually restricting his comments to how hard it was and to encourage her, "Don't give up!" Knowing she would encounter him, she'd have her tears wiped on her sleeve before meeting him—she still wept almost every time he saw her. He wondered why she let him see her cry, why she didn't walk another route back to her car, 'til he realised there was no other route that was private. So little by little the remarks between them in the rain-wet alley became more comfortable. He would even demonstrate, from time to time, with a broom handle, some technique. She began to know him as "Mr. Fujita" and he knew her name, "Emily." Sitting and smoking in the dark in front of Guan Yin, he fussed over the things he'd said to her. Why, he asked the god, do I have to speak with her? Guan Yin in her silence answered him over time. Emily is hiding, too.

Then, Fugitive did not see Emily for two weeks. At first he thought nothing of it. Studying for exams, he assumed. But, when he didn't see her for a third week, an instinct from his former life, sensitive to the rhythms of his watch, made him curious. He visited the local branch of the library and leafed through a few issues of the small, Japanese-language weekly newspaper that serviced the area, where he learned Emily's dojo had been involved in a regional kendo tournament. Discreetly, impersonating in his body language an idle, old Japanese man, he dropped by the Japantown building where the dojo was, in an aerobics studio on the second floor. Through the window and using the mirrors along the walls he stood and watched the practice without being seen. He knew from looking at the dojo's web site that the instructors were all Japanese *yūdansha* and that the dojo had a second location at a college campus. He wondered how many *hakujin*—"white people"—practised at the Japantown dojo. He watched for a while, and it was everything he expected, a vigorous recreational kendo club with experienced members under the direction of skilled sensei. He did not see Emily at *keiko*, and he left before anyone could strike up conversation with him.

For several days, Fujita toiled over his suspicions and schemed over what he might do. He tried to imagine the already alien experience of an American girl attempting to practise kendo at the Japantown dojo and what her first experience at a kendo *taikai* would have been like. He was relieved when he saw Emily coming down the alley again. But, he was struck by the seriousness in her face, the lack of her usual tears. Still, it made speaking to her easier—each recognised that the other had come to say something. Fujita spoke first. "Emily-san. I have not seen you in a while. Did you fight in the tournament?"

She nodded and smiled with embarrassment. "Fujita-san, I was terrible."

He was studying her face carefully, his suspicions growing more tangible in what he read there. He carefully, against his own impulses, laid a hand on her shoulder. "Emily-san, why don't you come in for a while? Let's have some tea, and talk about it. Maybe… you want to quit kendo?"

A hot rush of air leapt from Emily's chest into her mouth, was trapped behind her teeth, forced two hot, pink tears to appear in her eyes' corners. She nodded. "Come into the restaurant", Fujita insisted. "Let's talk about it." His nerve began to fail him. "Forgive me. Let's talk—I can encourage." He'd had this word ready, had looked up it and a few others in his Japanese-English dictionary. "Come in. Let's sit."

At the little table upstairs where he usually took his meals, while the restaurant mildly hummed below them, Fujita laid out a teapot, cups, some mandarin oranges. "What did your sensei say? Your senpai?"

"Sensei said nothing," Emily said. "Sometimes I think he doesn't even notice me, or maybe it's too awkward for him to speak to me. My senpai told me to just keep trying. Everybody just seems so embarrassed. Fujita-san, I felt like such a fool. I always feel like a fool but this was the worst." She described her match, how she became paralysed with apprehension, flailed and leapt stutteringly with her *shinai* until, after a few seconds, her opponent mercifully caught her rhythm and dispatched her with quick strikes to *men* and *kote*. "You know I have a problem with crying," she said, and seemed relieved to say it aloud to someone—the tears she had been fighting actually vanished in the chuckle that accompanied her admission. "I had to hold it in with all my might while I thanked my opponent and then slunk off to the side to take off my *men*. I cried like a baby in the toilet—someone thought I was vomiting. And that was the women's division. Then I had to do it all over again for *mudansha*. Thank God they didn't put me on a team."

As Emily spoke, Guan Yin's design became apparent to Fujita. He saw the angle at which their lives intersected. Emboldened, conscious that he needed to be getting back to work, Fujita said, "Emily-san, please don't quit kendo. Or, before you decide to quit, try again. Then, if you still don't like it, you can quit. But, let me help you. Let me give you extra practice."

Once Upon a Time in Japantown

If he was reading her face correctly, it said she was grateful for the encouragement, gladdened by his confidence in her, but apprehensive about what this "extra practice" might be. "You mean you'll come to the dojo?"

Fujita shook his head. "There is an empty storeroom in the basement of my apartment building in Japantown, with a wooden floor we can use." He told her the address. "I think maybe you need to train where you can take more time, where you are not surrounded by people better than you, that you have to keep up with. I'll help you. Just some basic practice. Not so much pressure. We can meet early morning before work. One hour. I promise you I will help you improve. And you won't have to quit kendo. Then", he added hopefully, "go to Japan, keep practising kendo with Japanese friends."

There was no turning back now, for either of them. She had left open the door for his counsel and he had let himself in, farther than either of them intended. But the bargain in the light of that evening didn't seem so bad, and anyway it could always be dissolved if it yielded no fruit, right? Fugitive hid behind his lock of hair. The clouds passed from Emily's face. "All right, sensei. What day?"

"Saturday. Eight o'clock."

There was, Fujita thought, nothing fundamentally wrong with Emily's basic movements except a lack of crispness and an acumen that could only be obtained by experience. Perhaps, there was a certain lack of confidence, too. But she wore her *bōgu* correctly and could hold *kamae* and cut *men* and *kirikaeshi* in a manner appropriate to her level—at least the level he imagined appropriate to a foreign-born beginner of kendo. For their first few meetings in the cramped, dusty storeroom, in which possessions that belonged to the residents of the building were held in small lockers with caged, padlocked doors, he did little except run her through her paces, offering a suggestion or two. He encouraged her—told her exactly what he thought: "You do well for someone that has just taken up kendo as an adult." He asked her if she knew the "small" *waza*. She did, though again not as well as she would if she kept practising for a few years. He gave her more pointers, dredging them up from deep within his memory and trying to match them to the present circumstance. He had never taught anyone like this before, someone that was new to the art, and it had been a long time since he himself was a beginner, so he was inventing what he needed, exploring.

The *bōgu* he wore was new, and stiff. He had thought about buying it at the little martial arts supply in the covered mall, but he was fearful it might draw attention to him. Instead, he ordered it on the internet using a computer at the library and a credit card he kept only for the purpose of obtaining housing and transportation and paying various, necessary bills. Donning the *bōgu*, swinging the new *shinai* over his head in the dusty basement that smelled of oil and damp concrete, he heard the fibrous creaks deep in his bones and felt scales of rust fall from him in tiny showers. He struck Emily, exchanged drills with her. She could receive the blows as well as deliver them.

After practice, Emily insisted on taking him to coffee at a little Japanese shop, where they could sit facing the sidewalk and engage in polite, idle talk over small cups and pastries. She could practise her Japanese, and they could watch the other shops open, the sun rounding the buildings and finding its tentative way into the streets like a drunk returning home.

It was helpful to her, but they were circling each other. Having taken stock of her basic ability in kendo, he now invited her to take free practice with him. In the narrow, subterranean space they bowed. Stepped forward. Drew blades. Dropped into *sonkyo*. The old radiance ascended with him. He held his powers in check. Challenged her with *kiai*. She answered, brave, but without confidence. Struck his unprotected *men*. Good. Now he would push her further. He edged forward, toward her throat. Raised his sword to strike.

She froze.

Now it became apparent. Again and again, as he struck her, she would pause, and flinch, and vaguely raise her *shinai*, to protect herself, and would be struck by him. Even when he raised as if to strike, but stopped, she was stuck—maybe she would cut at him as an afterthought but she had lost her opportunity and momentum. Now he stopped and invited her to attack him and she flailed weakly against him, only tapped his *men* or thrust at him weakly. He saw now that for all her fundamental skill, it was lost in the terror and confusion of an actual opponent.

At the coffee shop, she was jovial but he could see she was embarrassed. He was eager to assure her she had done nothing wrong. "I think I can now give some good advice about the trouble you are having in kendo", he said. He had been thinking of his words since they'd finished that morning's practice, and now he chose them, carefully, in English. "Emily, it is the normal way of being human to protect yourself when you are attacked. Even other martial arts teaches this, like karate or jujutsu. You raise your hands to protect your face and your body.

"But, in kendo, there is not this kind of defence. You could say, there is no defence—only attack. Even the advanced moves, the countering moves that look like defence, are a kind of attack. Anyway. Especially at your level you should only think of the attack. You should attack, even if it means you will be struck. You must give this up, the desire to protect yourself. Let yourself be struck. And, maybe this is the most difficult. You have to complete your attack, no matter what. Even if the opponent cuts you or will beat you, complete your attack. This is what we will concentrate on now. *Ai-uchi*—both opponents attacking each other at once." Fujita banged his fists together. "This is what you must do to get better at kendo. Do you understand?"

For the next several Saturdays, as the warm summer mornings yielded veins of autumn cold, they practised almost nothing but *ai-uchi*. The lack of space in their murky dojo, the fact that they could barely move to the left or right, proved to be of some benefit. It kept Emily focused on cutting straight forward and not dodging, on aiming her attacks into his oncoming attacks like the intersection of two lines. In a short time, she stopped flinching when Fujita pressed his attack. With more effort, she could attack his *men* at the same time he attacked hers and complete the attack, her body slamming into his and bounding away. He gave her further instruction on *taiatari* and the correct way to display *zanshin*. She learned that if she strove to attack confidently and with all the skill and vigour she could muster, she could beat an attack, her *kensen* would find his men soundly while his went arcing past her left ear. "Good!" he would praise. "Good cut, Emily-san!" They turned their attention to *kote*.

Practising Japanese at the coffee shop afterward, the topics turned naturally toward Fujita's home in Japan. Where was he from? Tokyo. Was his family still there? Some. What family? A daughter, a son. Married? Separated. Why did he live in the U.S.? He preferred it here. What was his job in Japan—hospitality, she guessed. Elusively, he said, "…civil service." Is that why your English is so good? Yes, his job had given him opportunity to practise what he learned in school. And why did he work as a dishwasher in a Chinese restaurant? Thoughtfully, he explained that it was a "retirement job."

He came close, once, to telling Emily more of the truth. Sitting at the bar with Guan Yin, smoking, he thought how grateful it would be to relieve himself to her. He explained to Guan Yin that if he were to say something to Emily he would say… He would say that he had been a cop, and that he was no longer a cop not because of things he'd done but because of things he'd not done, things he had let happen. And he might say… That when some of the things he'd let happen were exposed that he had been made to accept perhaps a greater portion of the blame for them as a way of shielding others. And he would try to explain… But how could he explain? It's why he had moved away, why he would not allow himself to return or have contact, even with his children, why he lived his ghost's life at the restaurant and in his rooms in Japantown. It was why he could not speak these things aloud in the daylight at the coffee shop, but only imagine he spoke them to the goddess behind the bar, in the restaurant lit only by the glow of the aquarium where the goldfish circled.

When the snows began to gather in the eaves, when icicles began to form beneath the curved lintels, they mutually agreed that it was becoming too cold to practise in the unheated storeroom, and they would suspend their *asa-geiko* until spring. He saw her less then, did not linger in the alley smoking cigarettes to encounter her on the way home from practice. But she dropped by the restaurant from time to time for tea. She let slip during one of these visits that another tournament was approaching and that she would participate, and that she was nervous and she hoped she would remember everything he had taught her. Sometime after that, she burst into the back door of the restaurant kitchen while he was elbow deep in hot, soapy water to tell him, "Sensei! Sensei! The tournament was last weekend!"

"And?" he blurted, happily surprised. "Did you win?"

"Win? No!" she answered. "But, I didn't suck!"

"Suck?" The context of the word in American English momentarily evaded him.

She answered in Japanese. "I did not win, but my performance was not poor. I was not embarrassed. I was not ashamed."

She was not ashamed. Goddess of Mercy.

Musō Jikiden Eishin-ryū Riai
The Meaning of the Kata: Part 2

By Kim Taylor

Introduction

This is Part 2 of a series of articles about the meaning behind the *kata* of the Musō Jikiden Eishin-ryū (MJER) and the organization of those *kata* into their levels and order. I claim no special knowledge of the thoughts of Ōe Masamichi as I was not alive when he reorganised the school into its present order. I simply offer my thoughts on this from a background of 30 years of practice in this school and in some other Japanese sword arts. Please understand while you are reading this that this is one person's way of organising and understanding the material. You are encouraged to read this, compare it with what you have been taught and what you understand, and come to your own conclusions.

Saya-banare on turns

On the turn and cut it is actually impossible to draw exactly to the opponent's centre from the outset. As the *tsuka* is moved into position, *saya-banare* (the moment at which the tip is snapped out of the *saya* and toward the target) should occur as the *tsukagashira* crosses the opponent's near shoulder. As you turn right in Hidari, *saya-banare* occurs as the *tsuka* points at the opponent's right shoulder. Start tightening your grip at this point so that by the time your hips are square and your right hand is centred on the opponent's *suigetsu*, your *monouchi* reaches the opponent's right shoulder. This is easiest to teach in Hidari, but the same happens when turning to the left in Migi, so it must be included in that *kata*. *Saya-banare* occurs as the *tsuka* points at the opponent's left shoulder and the right hand grip is closed. Therefore, when the turn is completed and the right hand is centred on the *suigetsu*, the *monouchi* has reached the opponent's right shoulder so that the cut can begin immediately.

There are many points that can be learned during this draw toward the opponent. There are also a large number of *jūjutsu* techniques to counter different angles of the draw. Two basic teachings about the draw are represented by the one described above and by a draw which moves to the front right used by many lines of the Musō Shinden-ryū.

Drawing directly toward the attacker with the *tsukagashira* pointed at the opponent's eyes as you release the tip of the blade from the *saya*, as described above, is done for the same reason a sticky pole is pushed directly at a bird when trying to catch it: It is very difficult to figure out how far away the *tsuka* is when seen end-on. Additionally, the most common way for an opponent to stop the draw is to grab the *tsuka*. If the opponent grabs the *tsuka* as it moves directly toward their face, it is hard for them to apply pressure to stop the draw. Even if they do manage to stop the forward movement, it is still not hard to complete the draw—drop the left hip back and move the *saya*, and then cut around the opponent's grip and let the *tsuka* pivot on their hand as the cut is made.

Drawing to the right front, as is done in many lines of the Musō Shinden-ryū, is to protect the right wrist with the *tsuka* during the draw. One of the secrets of both schools, which used to be reserved for experienced students, is the draw and cut of the opponent's right wrist rather than the deeper cut to their face or chest. Another reason to draw to the front right is that it opens and exposes the blade edge to the opponent's hand as they reach to grab the *tsuka* and prevent the draw. A third reason is that drawing at this angle allows the *tsuka* to be thrown forward to cut the face or shoulder of the opponent, or for the *tsuka* to be pulled back and the tip of the blade aimed at the opponent for a thrust.

As you can see, this opening movement of the very first *kata* can be used to teach many lessons regarding the draw and attack from the *saya*. That many lines have many different versions of this draw should remind us that *kata* are places of study rather than fixed responses to fixed attacks. However, this is how beginners are taught.

Ushiro

When dealing with an opponent who is directly behind you (*ma-ushiro*), you cannot draw directly toward them. In this case you must move the *tsuka* a little to one side before you can move your hand directly at the opponent's centre. The question is how far to draw as you turn to the side and which way do you turn? A second consideration is how to turn 180 degrees without alerting the opponent too early. All of this is accomplished by sliding the right knee to the left, and then forward until the right knee is ahead of the left. Because of a two fist-width distance between the knees, this works to take your pivoting knee to the proper position, so you just turn on the right knee and left foot to move into position. To reiterate, the feet are touching at the toes, and the knees are two fists apart so there is a V-shape to the legs. You move one leg of the V to the other and leave the left foot in the centre, as the left foot rolls over it moves to the side by a foot-width. The result of all this is that there is no further need to shift the foot and you are facing directly behind yourself. The draw begins as you turn but it does not go too far to

USHIRO

Ushiro-nuki

the side. As soon as there is a direct line from right hand to the target, draw directly along that line using a strong *saya-biki*, as in Migi.

The distance to the opponent and which way to turn at 180 degrees

To examine what is happening in these *kata*, you should consider where the opponent is and how far away he is. This distance is decided by assuming that you cut across the shoulders as you reach the *nuki-tsuke* position. So for Mae, to work out the correct spacing, get into *nuki-tsuke* and touch your training partner on the right shoulder at the correct distance with a *bokutō*. This is roughly one *bokutō*'s length between the knees while sitting in *seiza*. After finding this position you can see where you would be hitting with two hands in *kiri-tsuke*. The distance does not need to be much nearer, and only a very small shift is needed if your opponent drops back down into *seiza*. Your opponent can try to stand and move backward if he wishes, and you will find that you do not need to chase him to perform the final strike on target unless you are very slow.

For Migi and Hidari, the distance would, once again, be around a *bokutō* from knee to knee. For Ushiro you will see that the distance is once again from knee to knee, not knee to foot as you might imagine. This supposes that the opponent is not driving forward towards us, but only rises onto his knees. Would an opponent sit this close to you and try to attack from this distance? Try it and see.

Another possibility is to go with the first idea and put the opponent a sword-length from your feet to his knees. Now, imagine that he is going to reach for your *saya* from behind. Assuming you start to rise and turn to avoid his grasp, in which direction is it best to turn? If you turn clockwise to your right, you see that the *saya* disappears away from the opponent immediately so it would seem this course of action would be best. This would probably indicate to a beginner that the *kata* is incorrect. Try it. You, as the opponent, lunge for the *saya*. It is gone, and now the opponent is turning toward you leading with his right elbow. You are close enough to jam that elbow and prevent him from attacking.

Now, in the role of the swordsman, try moving counter clockwise toward the opponent as he reaches for your *saya*, as you are required to do in the *kata*. The opponent reaches for the *saya* but it moves across his body. He will follow it to the right while you are approaching him on the left side. Even if he gives up and tries to jam you, can you prevent him from doing that while driving this way?

You will find that you can continue your hip turn and strip the *saya* from the blade even if he avoids grabbing the edge of the blade and has hold of your *tsuka*. You can then strike around the *tsuka* to cut him in the shoulder. There will be more talk of the jujutsu of the sword when discussing the Eishin-ryū. Students in the role of the opponent can try interfering with the draw rather than drawing their own sword for the first three *kata* now. The ideas introduced in our discussion of *saya-banare* during the turns will provide useful material for research.

All Directions for all Kata

With practice in these four *kata* (or one *kata* practised from four directions) you can now attack in any direction and students should feel free to practise at any angle they wish. The first three *kata* seem perfectly obvious; you drive straight in or turn the shortest distance toward the opponent to attack. However, when do you switch from clockwise to counter-clockwise if you keep turning left and put the opponent between 90 degrees and 180 degrees to your right? Examine when the "shortest distance" loses out to "an opening to control the elbow".

You will see another instance of one *kata* from multiple directions again, but it is not necessary to repeat the lesson too often. You should try every *kata* from multiple directions and see which will work and which are limited in their application toward different directions.

Yae Gaki

I would now like to discuss the *kae-waza* of this technique first as it is a very logical progression from the first four techniques. The *kata* starts with a *nuki-tsuke* like in Mae, but as the opponent scrambles backward, you simply step forward with the left foot and cut him down vertically. You then do *yoko-chiburi* (a horizontal movement of the sword to the right) and then put the blade away while moving back into a *tate-hiza* position with the right knee down and the left knee up. As the *nōtō* is almost done another opponent attacks from the front and you stand while pulling the left foot further back, cutting horizontally and then vertically to finish the second opponent.

It is clear that this is simply Mae done forward and then backward along the same line. What is important here is to understand that you are moving backward not out of *seiza*, but out of a raised knee position where it is much easier to perform a backward movement. For a beginner, this may be your first exposure to *tate-hiza*, which will

YAE GAKI

Yae Gaki-nuki

Yae Gaki-kiri *Yae Gaki-chiburi*

Yae Gaki-nōtō

Yae Gaki-nuki

be used throughout the next two levels of practice.

In the standard version of this technique, the second horizontal cut is replaced by a downward block against an attack to the ankle by the fallen opponent. After this block you move forward again to finish the opponent with a vertical cut through the body. If you can perform this block you can certainly do the *nuki-tsuke kae-waza*. Consequently, some lines only practise this version of the technique.

This technique is a transition out of the basic *kata* (Mae or 1-4) that introduces a simple iaido sequence to the student while getting them used to moving around from *seiza*. The block and the idea of multiple attacks or a defensive movement is a hint of things to come. Try Yae Gaki from different angles and the *kae-waza* with the two opponents coming from two different directions.

Moving Back Out of Seiza

I noted above that it is hard to move backward from *seiza*. One way to do it is to flip the toes underneath and "pop" both knees off the floor into the *sonkyo* position, and then step back. It is not fast but it works. Because this is possible, a beginner will stand and cut down rather than scooting along on the floor with a knee-walking type motion. A more advanced student may wish to explore how to move around on the knees while using the sword. In this case, the right knee must be dropped to the ground to allow the left knee to rise and the left foot to move forward. Try this while keeping the hips pointed straight ahead, and while letting the hips swing around the pivot point of the knees.

Uke Nagashi

Your opponent approaches you from the left and is standing. He tries to cut down onto your head but you avoid by stepping forward with the left foot. The opponent then lifts his blade and immediately tries again to cut down onto your head. You move your right foot out to face him and deflect his blade to the left with your own drawn blade. You continue your movement and cut him down vertically while bringing your right foot up to the left.

Up to this point the attacks have begun with *sen-no-sen* timing, with an attack into an attack. Uke Nagashi introduces *go-no-sen* timing, with a distinct defensive movement before the counterattack. While this is not the first defence from the *saya* (all the draws above were defensive), it is the first time a distinct defensive movement is made to start the *kata*. In this case (at least as I practise it) there is a multiple attack in the form of two cuts—the first is avoided by moving forward onto the left foot; the second by continuing to move forward with the right foot while drawing and turning toward the opponent to catch his strike on your sword. The key here is the slipping forward to avoid the first strike, a technique that allows the swordsman a choice, to then turn and deflect, or to continue onward out the door and across the fields.

This will not be the last time you move to the side of the line of attack. Understanding the attack line is critical to swordplay and it should be thought about from the outset.

YAE GAKI

Yae Gaki-kiri

Yae Gaki-chiburi

Yae Gaki-nōtō

UKE NAGASHI

Uke Nagashi-nuki

Uke Nagashi-chiburi

Uke Nagashi-nōtō

KAISHAKU

Kaishaku-nuki

Kaishaku-chiburi   *Kaishaku-nōtō*

無雙直傳英信流居合術

Kaishaku

Why, if you are a student of the school, is this the seventh technique you learn? Actually, if you assume that the first four *kata* are really the same, why is this the fourth technique? This is something you should consider. Kaishaku has a different feel from the other *kata* and so emphasizes those differences and reinforces what you should be doing in the others as well. The cut is the first that deviates from what you have been taught so far. The shape is also quite different from other cuts, so you start at an early stage learning to control the blade movement while maintaining effectiveness. The shape is a result of the target being at waist height rather than your own height so the maximum distance forward for the blade is at a horizontal position. This results in an elliptical cut with a flat bottom.

Beginners are told that it is "in bad taste" to demonstrate this *kata* in public. This is true, but there are philosophical and ethical implications to this admonition. Think about why the demonstration of this *kata* should be considered private, while all others are allowed in public demonstrations.

TSUKE KOMI

Tsuke Komi-nuki

Tsuke Komi-kiri

Tsuke Komi-chiburi

Tsuke Komi-nōtō

Tsuke Komi

The opponent is standing and approaches from the front with his sword over his head. You bring your right foot forward while drawing and then avoid his strike by stepping back, and then forward again to cut him down with vertical strikes.

This *kata* begins as if you are drawing for Mae with every intention of cutting across the opponent's body if he stops his strike or does not otherwise take the bait—your head—which is moved toward him. If there is space, cut across the stomach. In other words, you are back to Mae. If you do not draw with full intent to cut, if you think of this movement as a fake, you will simply be cut down. This *kata* introduces the idea of presenting a target for the opponent to strike at, and then removing it. It is a form of *seme* to provoke a response so that you can attack the space created by the opponent's failed attack.

This is where the student begins to understand the limitations of the *seiza* posture and discovers that moving forward into the attack can create a space (in distance or time) and the proper leg position so that he can move backward to avoid a strike. In other words, to move backward efficiently it is a good idea to move from *seiza* into *tate-hiza*.

As you avoid the attack and counterattack toward the opponent's face, you must continue to exert *seme* to keep the opponent on their heels until you can perform the finishing cut. It is not hard for the opponent to avoid the first response cut from you, so the opponent must not be allowed to regain the initiative. This sort of dogged perseverance is always a good thing to learn.

TSUKI KAZE

Tsuki Kaze-nuki

Tsuki Kaze-kiri

Tsuki Kaze-chiburi

Tsuki Kaze-nōtō

Tsuki Kaze

The standing opponent moves in from the right, again in *jōdan*. You turn and draw to your right and cut across his forearms, then finish with a vertical cut.

While this *kata* may seem to be something new and exciting, it is simply Hidari to an opponent who is standing and attacking. You turn into and under the attack from the right, and instead of cutting horizontally, simply cut upward into the wrists. Shooting the right leg forward and staying very low allows you to reach the target before the opponent gets into range on his strike, just as his cut begins to drop. This technique has similarities to a variation of the Tachi Uchi no Kurai *kata*, Shin Myo Ken, where if the opponent has gone too far in his swing to cut his wrists, his sword can be attacked from the draw and knocked sideways to create the space for a counterattack.

From the first three *kata*, you have now seen an opponent attack from the left, centre and right, as well as from a standing position with sword already drawn in *jōdan*. From the perspective of an adult learner, this is a great way to make the first three *kata* seem easy.

OI KAZE

Oi Kaze-nuki

Oi Kaze-kiri

Oi Kaze-chiburi

Oi Kaze-nōtō

Oi Kaze

This is Mae while running forward. The opponent is facing you and tries to draw, but you take two quick steps forward to crowd his movement by getting inside his attack arc. This forces him to start moving backward to make space to draw. You follow him, but then allow him to move away from you until you have the space to draw and cut him just as he finds his range to draw and cut you. You will see the other side of this technique in Oku Iai in the *kata* Tora Bashiri. This principle of crowding in and then allowing the opponent to move back out to attack range is a very subtle use of *maai* and must be examined carefully in order to understand it fully.

The shuffling, short stride running style used in Oi Kaze is important to practise well as it provides a stable platform from which to draw and cut, as well as giving you the ability to draw at any point, to stop instantly, and to keep the feet close to the ground so that power can be used most effectively. Bend the knees toward each other and examine the role of the hips in the movement.

A variation of this *kata* is to chase down and kill an opponent from behind who is running away. However, that is a principle best reserved for levels of training beyond the beginner, and the technique (called *oi kaze-giri*) has been largely dropped from most lines of practice. Consider these two solo iaido *kata*, done essentially the same way, but the difference being an opponent who is running backward or one who is running away. Why would one be dropped from the curriculum? Is it simply a matter of getting rid of duplicate material, or is there a deeper lesson here?

NUKI UCHI

Nuki Uchi-nuki

Nuki Uchi-chiburi

Nuki Uchi-nōtō

無雙直傳英信流居合術

Nuki Uchi

There is no more basic demonstration of *iai* than Nuki Uchi, a finishing cut directly from the *saya*. This *kata* is seen in all three levels of practice and is presented in a progressive manner with the Ōmori-ryū version being the simplest of the three, a draw to the side to avoid potential interference by the opponent, a rise over the head through an *uke-nagashi* position and a cut down with both hands while splitting the knees to drop the weight into the cut. This is taught to beginners as *sen-sen-no-sen*, an attack just as the opponent decides to attack, and in the upper levels of practice, this principle will be more and more apparent. It is revealing that this *kata* is taught more as *sen-no-sen* and even as *go-no-sen* to more advanced students. The *sen-sen-no-sen* aspect makes it easy for beginners to understand. The opponent has not moved and you are performing a "pre-emptive defence", or as some would say, a "sneak attack". As the skill level of the student rises, subtle changes in the *kata* are introduced that allow it to fall into the more conventional defensive modes, along with the rest of the *kata* in the set.

What Ōmori Teaches

This first set of *kata* represents the basic instruction in the Musō Jikiden Eishin-ryū, one opponent at a time with simple attacks. In the rest of the sets you will build on this foundation of simple patterns. With a horizontal cut from the *saya* and a vertical finishing cut combined with different angles of strike (higher than your head, down below your knee) and moving in different directions, you can perform hundreds of variations. By including what has been discussed here, you can also create compound responses to many unusual attacks.

Philosophy

The underlying theory of this set is "*saya no uchi no kachi*", or "winning in the scabbard". While drawing toward the opponent you must be thinking "don't draw". In the *sen-no-sen kata*, at any point between starting the draw and *saya-banare*, if the opponent backs down you do not finish your draw. Once *saya-banare* is reached, you cut. Most of the *kata* in this set allow you to follow this ideal. The *go-no-sen kata* of Uke Nagashi and Tsuke Komi might be considered as starting as the opponent attacks, but both contain a small opportunity just before the blade is released from the *saya* where the opponent has a chance to stop attacking. The one apparent exception to this rule is the *sen-sen-no-sen* version of Nuki Uchi, which has been discussed.

What this is then, is a beginning set that, from a philosophical and ethical viewpoint, firmly establishes a deep reluctance to simply cut down an opponent even if given the reason, means and opportunity to do so. This ethical aspect to the art will continue through the remaining levels of the school, although the point of decision changes and the ethical challenge to the student becomes more complex.

Part 3 of this series will continue in *Kendo World* 8.1 with a look at the Chūden teachings of the Eishin-ryū techniques.

BOOK REVIEW

Encyclopedia of Japanese Martial Arts

by David A. Hall
Reviewed by Antony Cundy

The fact that Kendo World has not yet reviewed this book is quite an oversight, as it is a seminal document in the serious study of budo. For the first time an academically, as well as physically, experienced practitioner has gathered together, from the full spectrum of Japanese martial arts, a trove of information to act as a resource for both the scholar and amateur. It is truly encyclopaedic.

Dr. David Hall, has spent 45 years training in the martial arts, both in their modern and classical incarnations. In addition, ordained as a Tendai priest in 1978, his religious training is in clear view as the sections referring to the religious and philosophical elements of budo are exceptional. Until now Dr. Hall has been relatively quiet in terms of publishing. Aside from articles for JMAS and the International Hoplological Society his most famous work was his PhD thesis from the University of California, "Marishiten: Buddhism and the Warrior Goddess", later published under the title *The Buddhist Goddess Marishiten: A Study of the Evolution and Impact of Her Cult on the Japanese Warrior* (Global International / Brill Academic).

The individual entries, in the total of 4,000, range from the erudite and functional, such as;

dan 段: 1. Lit. "step", "level", or "grade". See; dan-kyu. 2. A term for the division of kata sets in the Jigen-ryū 示現流

to the vaguely fetishistic;

nokogiribiki 鋸引: Lit. "Sawing the throat". Nokogiribiki was one of the four prescribed forms of execution for Tokugawa Period commoners. See: Shikei.

Whether this particular entry has a home in a book on budo is up for discussion. However, each is given the same scholarly treatment and one can spend profitable time simply following themes from one entry's notes to another.

Dr. Hall is certainly more comfortable in certain areas which are indicative of his personal experience. The entries pertaining to Kashima Shinden Jikishinkage-ryū, Shindō Musō-ryū, Marishiten and Buddhism are clearly more authoritative. The sections referring to Katori Shintō-ryū are also notable, perhaps reflecting the close relationship between the author and the late scholar/practitioner, Donn F. Draeger.

There are some unusually light entries. Specifically, the section on Miyamoto Musashi, likely the first person a non-Japanese would state when asked to name a famous Japanese historical figure. His section amounts to only 16 lines in comparison with the more obscure Hirano Kuniomi, practitioner of the Shindō Musō-ryū, who was granted 38. I was also surprised not to see an entry for Sugino Yoshio, Katori Shintō-ryū master and swordsmanship advisor to Akira Kurosawa in such films as *The Seven Samurai*. Also notably missing are Gōjū-ryū's Higaonna Morio and Hatsumi Masaaki of ninjutsu fame.

From a purely selfish point of view the section on Suiei-jutsu was also weak, neither noting the existing 13 traditions or indeed referring to them by the standard terms of Nihon Eihō or Suijutsu. There are also a few typos, such as Suiō-ryū being referred to as Kenpō Iai rather than Iai Kenpō.

However, let me be very clear in stating that in a book of this scale such mistakes are inevitable. The sheer volume of entries and the exceptionally well organised contents, from lineage charts to curriculum descriptions, is outstanding. Dr. Hall has curated and created a book that deserves to be on the bookshelf of every modern library, private and public, achieving its stated purpose, to 'provide an introduction to classical combative terminology and provide a foundation for more advanced study of Japan's classical martial culture.'

This brings me to a thought. In the age of the shared economy and Wikipedia, I believe that using Dr. Hall's encyclopaedia as a starting point we have the chance to move the level of academic rigour in the history of the arts we study forward greatly. Indeed, I would personally ask Dr. Hall to act as the curator and editor for succeeding volumes, to expand and evolve this clearly epic undertaking. A reprinting every five years would be an opportunity to bring more information to the fore and centralise references. I can think of nobody more qualified to lead this and frankly, after the sheer hard work that must have gone into this first edition, nobody who deserves it more.

Encyclopedia of Japanese Martial Arts is available through Kodansha USA, ISBN 978-1-56836-410-0.

Thoughts on *Monouchi* and *Datotsu-bu*

By Dr. Sergio Boffa

Definitions

Monouchi and *datotsu-bu* are two important Japanese terms frequently used in kendo training and competitions. They seem to be synonymous, but this is not actually the case as each term has a specific meaning. Therefore, a clear understanding of these terms is of great importance. The purpose of this paper is to clearly define the terms "*monouchi*" and "*datotsu-bu*" as a precise definition of them is not easily found.

First, an examination of the etymology of these two words. *Monouchi* is a combination of two Chinese characters (*kanji*). The first means "thing" or "object" (物, *mono*) and the second "to hit" (打つ, *utsu*). Consequently, the *monouchi* means "the object that strikes an object". *Datotsu-bu* is a group of three *kanji*. The first two are "to strike" (打つ, *utsu*) and "to thrust" or "to stab" (突く, *tsuku*), and these form the word "attack". The last *kanji* means "part" or "portion" (部, *bu*). Therefore, the *datotsu-bu* is the portion of the blade that is used to attack. Thus, these two terms seem to have an almost identical meaning.

More about their differences can be learned from the *Japanese-English Dictionary of Kendo*, edited by the All Japan Kendo Federation (AJKF), which states that the *monouchi* is "the part of the blade of the sword which cuts the best, it is said to be located about 10cm from the tip. In the case of the *shinai*, it refers to the part of the *jinbu* where force is used most efficiently, and it is the region between the tip and the *nakayui*" (fig. 4).[1]

This simple definition is ambiguous. On a sword, the *monouchi* would be a very short area—maybe a single point—located about 10cm from the tip (*kensen*), but on a *shinai* it runs from the *nakayui* to the *kensen*. It would then cover several tens of centimetres since it is advisable to attach the *nakayui* at a quarter of the total length of the *shinai*, about 30cm, from the tip. It will be seen that this inconsistency is neither a mistake nor innocent.

The same dictionary states that the *datotsu-bu* is "the part of the *shinai* with which one should strike the opponent. Refers to the *jinbu* (side opposite the *tsuru*) around the region of the *monouchi*"[2] or "the name of a part of the *shinai*. It is the part with which one should strike the opponent and refers to the *jinbu* (side opposite the *tsuru*) around the region of the *monouchi*. For *tsuki*, it refers to the tip of the *shinai*."[3]

These two definitions suggest that the *datotsu-bu* is a large area which includes the *monouchi*. This is confirmed by another text, the referee's manual, also published by the AJKF: "[The] *datotsu-bu* of *shinai* shall be *jinbu* of *monouchi* and its neighbouring part".[4]

The illustrations present in these different books do not clarify the situation. The drawing of the *shinai* in the first edition of the dictionary and in the referee's manuals of 2000 and 2006 put the *monouchi* just below the *nakayui*.[5] In the second edition of the dictionary as well as in the 1996 referee's manual, this area is slightly moved toward the *kensen*.[6] In the last edition of the dictionary, the *monouchi* is located between the *nakayui* and the *kensen*.[7]

These variations are surprising, but they are not the result of intense brain storming made by the theoreticians at the AJKF. It seems obvious that the erroneous positioning of the illustration legends is the main cause for the misplacement of that area.

Note that only the latest edition of the dictionary represents the location of the *monouchi* on a katana. It is much smaller and is near one-fifth of the length of the blade (fig. 3.1 a).[8] Curiously, the first two editions of the dictionary seem to judge this precision superfluous.

At first glance, this investigation into the definition of the *monouchi* may seem futile, but this is not the case. The dictionary refers to an area "which cuts the best" or "where force is used most efficiently".[9] It is true that there is an area of maximum efficiency on a sword. Let us examine how science determines the true *monouchi* and if it fits the official definition of *monouchi*.

The centre of percussion

On a blade there is a special point called the "centre of percussion". Its position is determined according to a rotation point set, in this case, by the place in which the weapon is held. Therefore, the rotation point is usually located at the level of the left fist or in the middle of the hilt (*tsuka*) depending on how *waza* are performed.

Why is the centre of percussion important? When we hit a target with a sword, the weapon is under the action of several forces; forces that vary depending on the place of the impact:

(1) If the impact takes place above the centre of percussion, the blade will bend down. The user will have the impression that the hilt will crush their fingers (fig. 1.1).
(2) If the impact takes place below the centre of percussion, the upper part of the blade will bend upwards. The user will have the impression that the handle pushes back into the palm (fig. 1.2).
(3) If the impact takes place right on the centre of percussion, all the forces vanish and the hands will suffer no shock at all (fig. 1.3).

From a purely scientific point of view, the centre of percussion is a specific point. But, pragmatically, to strike with neighbouring areas will offer virtually the same effect to the user.

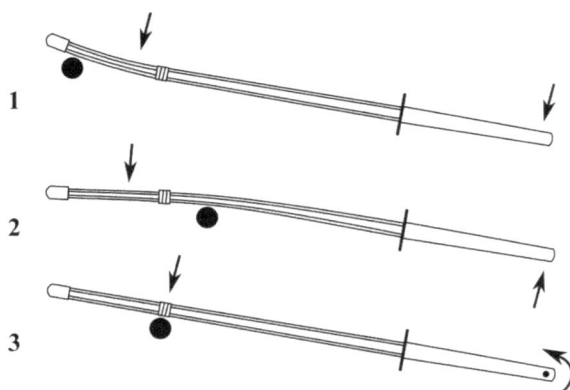

Fig. 1 Reactions of the shinai during an impact

The nodes of vibration

The nodes of vibration also play an important role. A sword (*nihontō*), *bokutō* and *shinai* are not fully rigid, and they vibrate when they receive a shock. The degree of vibration depends on the length of the weapon and its rigidity. The lowest frequency is called the 1st harmonic (or fundamental frequency). The others are the 2nd and the 3rd harmonic (or 1st and 2nd overtones) (fig. 2). According to these frequencies, there are several nodes of vibration on a blade, and a shock at one of them does not make the blade vibrate. The further away from a vibration node a blade is struck, the stronger the vibrations will be, but even if the vibrations become significant, the nodes remain at rest. It will be shown that this characteristic plays an important role in the conception of a sword.

These vibrations represent a loss of energy, which means that a part of the force will not be transmitted to the target and will be wasted. They are also felt by the user, making it less comfortable. It is therefore preferable to avoid them.

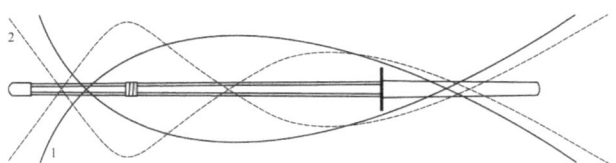

Fig. 2 Nodes of vibration
  1. 1st harmonic
  2. 2nd harmonic

Note that this figure is a simple schema. We do not have the tools needed to obtain scientific data to accurately represent the vibrations of a *shinai*.

In the case of a Japanese sword, vibration nodes theoretically must be placed where the right hand takes the weapon. Thus, regardless of the place on the blade which is excited, vibrations will be lower or null there. It seems that it is the ideal place to position the small holes (*mekugi-ana*) on the tang (*nakago*). Thus, a small piece of bamboo or metal (*mekugi*) will suffer less tension. Yet this does not seem to have been the concern of Japanese craftsmen. Although these holes are often found on the tang of old blades, being able to equip a blade with several mountings (*koshirae*) seemed to be more important than the behaviour of the weapon in combat.

In the case of a *shinai*, it would have been more interesting to place them inside the left hand. But because the sword is grabbed at the end of the hilt, it is not physically possible without altering the shape of the *shinai*.

The area of maximum efficiency—The science

It has been demonstrated that the *monouchi* is the area of maximum efficiency. Such a zone, also called "sweet spot" or "sweet zone", exists on a sword or any other handheld tool. The location of the centre of percussion and vibration nodes define that zone. In the case of a baseball bat or a tennis racket, scientific debate still rages about which of these points is the most important.[10] As they are very close, at least on the sports instruments mentioned above, this debate is of no real importance and the "sweet zone" is located virtually in the same place regardless of which one of these points we favour.

George L. Turner, who became interested in the physics of the sword, thinks that only the centre of percussion should be taken into account.[11] At the end of the nineteenth century, when swords and sabres were still being used on the battlefield, the engineers in charge of designing these weapons believed so, too.[12] Pending new scientific studies on the sweet zone of a sword, it will therefore be considered as being the determining factor, and the *monouchi* should therefore lie around that point.

If it is possible to find the accurate location of the centre of percussion and the vibration nodes, the calculus and measurements involved are nevertheless relatively complex to perform on an object such as a *shinai*, *bokutō* or *nihontō*. Fortunately, experimentation can help them to be located, with some precision, on these different tools.

To find the position of the centre of percussion, gently hit the blade all along from the *kensen* to the *tsuba* in order to discover where shocks in the hand are null or very weak. If the blade is flexible, it is easy to discover the position of the node of the 2nd harmonic. Hit the tang or hilt violently and observe the place located on the side of the tip which does not vibrate.

The area of maximum efficiency—The data

Now, after the scientific view, let us examine what sword users think about the area of maximum efficiency.[13] The traditional school Musō Jikiden Eishin-ryū proposes an unusual method to find the beginning of the *monouchi*. Place the back of the sword (*mune*), near the handle (*tsubamoto*), on the edge of a table. The blade is held in this position, edge upward, at an angle of approximately 45°. Let the blade slide naturally toward you. At one point, the sword will turn and have its cutting edge facing downwards. This is where the *monouchi* begins and it continues until the *kensen*. Usually, it is the upper third of the blade. For the Nakamura-ryū, a school of *battōdō*, the *monouchi* is the second sixth of the blade. In the case of a 75cm blade, it is the area between 12.5cm and 25cm (fig. 3.1 b).[14]

It can be seen that these two schools do not agree on either where to find the *monouchi* or its length. Can these methods be compared with the scientific experiments mentioned above? After several tests on a *nihontō*, *bokutō* and *shinai*, it was found that:

1) On a modern *nihontō*,[15] the centre of percussion is about 23cm from the tip, i.e. close to a third of the length of the cutting edge (72cm) and a quarter of the total length of the blade (94cm) (fig. 3.1). The method proposed by the Muso Jikiden Eishin-ryū school (fig. 3.1 c) was also tested. Surprisingly, the blade starts to turn around 30 cm (fig. 3.1 d) and stands on the cutting edge only at around 10cm from the tip (fig. 3.1 e).
2) On the *bokutō*, the centre of percussion is approximately 25cm from the tip, i.e. a third of the

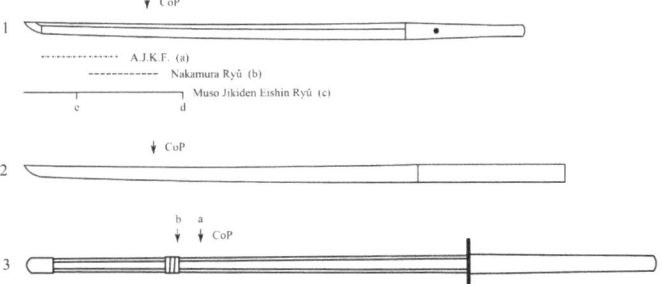

Fig. 3 Location of the centre of percussion on a nihontō (1), a bokutō (2) and a shinai (3).

length of the cutting edge (75cm) and a quarter of the total length of the weapon (101cm) (fig. 3.2).

3) On a *shinai* (bamboo) the centre of percussion is around 34cm from the tip (fig. 3.3 a). [16] This is no longer in the proportions of one third of the blade or one quarter of the weapon (118cm), but between one-quarter and one-third (118/34 = 3.47). If the proportions had been maintained, the centre of percussion would have been located at 29.5cm from the tip (fig. 3.3 b). This distance from the *kensen* is normal. The *nihontō* and *bokutō* have a relatively uniform mass distribution. Bamboo, on the other hand, usually has a lot more weight on the side of the *tsuka* than the *kensen*.

And the datotsu-bu in all of this?

A lot of time has been spent looking at what the *monouchi* is. If we keep the official definition from the AJKF—the part of the cutting edge (*jinbu*) extending from the *kensen* to the *naka-yui* [17]—then one wonders why we are asked to refer to the *datotsu-bu* when it comes to refereeing. Fortunately, this can be easily explained.

First, the part with which the target (*datotsu-bui*) must be hit slightly changes depending on the attack. Thus, if men is the reference, it is possible to score an *ippon* by touching the *kote* with a part of the blade much closer to the *kensen*. In the case of the *dō*, a wide area close to the middle of the blade is still acceptable. The *datotsu-bu* is therefore not linked to the proprieties of a blade, but according to the way in which the sword is used, i.e. the choice of *waza*.

Second, the *monouchi* is not related at all to the *tsuki* attack since its *datotsu-bu* is located at the tip of the *sakigawa* (fig. 4).

The definition of the *monouchi* is therefore far too restrictive to be used by a *shinpan* during a *shiai*. This is why the term *datotsu-bu* is used and why it is described as an area situated "around" the *monouchi*. Unfortunately, all this indicates is that a better understanding of the

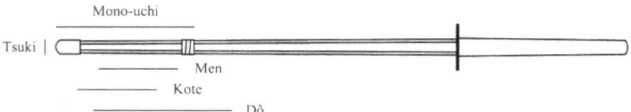

Fig. 4 The different datotsu-bu according to different attacks

datotsu-bu will not help us to have a better understanding of what the *monouchi* is.

Conclusions

The "true *monouchi*" can be precisely located on a weapon since it is the area of maximum efficiency. The "experimental *monouchi*" proposed by some schools like the Nakamura-ryū or Muso Jikiden Eishin-ryū is not consistent with science, and neither is the official definition proposed by the AJKF. There is clearly no consensus between scientists, kendoka or other swordsmen. How and why is this possible?

Do these differences mean that kendo masters do not have a clear idea of what the *monouchi* is? Yes and no. Swordsmen of the past were naturally incapable of understanding the scientific laws that explain the presence of an area of maximum efficiency. They nevertheless discovered its existence empirically. This empirical knowledge is still used today, for example, during the practice of the Nippon Kendo Kata. It is at the level of the centre of percussion that one should hit the forehead of their partner (fig. 5). Problems arise when these kendoka have to realise or materialise their knowledge with words.

Fig. 5 Nippon Kendo Kata - Ippon-me

In the case of a real sword, some practitioners seem to consider the centre of percussion as marking the beginning of the *monouchi*, while it should actually be at the middle of it. It is not, in my opinion, a simple imprecision. From a purely practical point of view, it is usually better to keep the adversary at a maximum distance. Therefore, if the centre of percussion lies at the first third of this blade (c. 25cm) and the area of maximum efficiency stands around this point, say c. 12.5 to c. 37.5 cm, it is better (or safer) to use the part of the blade ranging from 25cm to 12.5cm (to the point), rather than from 25cm to 37.5cm. This might explain some of the discrepancies between all of our definitions.

The case of the *shinai* is quite different. It is clear that hitting a target with the area of maximum efficiency provides various benefits:

—The *shinai* does not vibrate, which facilitates its control right after impact.
—The rotation point after the impact is located at the end of the *tsuka*, in the left hand. This also facilitates the control of the *shinai*, and makes it easier to maintain a correct posture during the phase of *zanshin*.
—Maximum force is transmitted to the target, which allows a better sharpness (*sae*) of the *waza*.

The true *monouchi* is therefore a useful area. Then why are official definitions contrary to the laws of physics (it would extend from the *kensen* to the *naka-yui* and this would be the part where the "force is used most efficiently" [18])? Remember that the centre of percussion is usually located at one third of the length of the blade, exactly where it is advised to tie the *naka-yui*. It is therefore impossible to use this part of the blade properly without risking damage to this thin piece of leather. The official location and length of the *monouchi* on a *shinai* are therefore arbitrary and do not correspond to any physical, historical or practical reality.

It is possible to explain what appears to be a gross mistake. The AJKF is not interested in which area of the bamboo would be the most effective when making a cut. After all, the *shinai* is not a weapon, a *shiai* is not a real fight, and nowadays, opponents are simply "hit", not "cut". Therefore, the official definition of the *monouchi* is just a pedagogical tool designed to remind practitioners what part of the blade we should use during an attack.

Furthermore, within the strict framework of training with a *shinai*, the last third of the blade is a kind of area of maximum efficiency since it is the part of the blade which allows us to launch the fastest attack at the greatest distance. If the authors of the dictionary did not add "where force is used most efficiently" their definition could be quite valid.

All these reflect the evolution of modern kendo well. The *shinai* is no longer a substitute for a real sword. It becomes a weapon with its own handling and techniques. Consequently, the AJKF had no other choice than to adapt old vocabulary and concepts to the use of this new tool.

End notes

1. This is what we call the "official *mono-uchi*" (*Dictionary of Kendo* (1996), p. 72; *Dictionary of Kendo* (2000), p. 65; *Dictionary of Kendo* (2011), p. 70).
2. *Dictionary of Kendo* (1996), p. 125.
3. *Dictionary of Kendo* (2000), p. 116; *Dictionary of Kendo* (2011), p. 118.
4. *The Regulations of Kendo Shiai* (2006), sect. 2, art. 13, p. 6.
5. *Dictionary of Kendo* (1996), p. 156; *The Regulations of Kendo Shiai*, p. 23
6. *Dictionary of Kendo* (2000), p. 150; *The Regulations of Kendo Shiai* (1996), p. 23.
7. *Dictionary of Kendo* (2011), p. 151.
8. *Ibid.*, p. 154.
9. *Dictionary of Kendo* (1996), p. 72; *Dictionary of Kendo* (2000), p. 65; *Dictionary of Kendo* (2011), p. 70.
10. Bibliography in Cross, R. *Physics of Baseball & Softball*, New York, 2011.
11. Turner, G.L. *Dynamics*, pp. 41-42, 131.
12. Latham, J. "The Shape of Sword Blades".
13. It is what we call the "experimental *monouchi*".
14. Nakamura, T. *The Spirit of the Sword*, pp. 56, 231; J.-P. Reniez, *Le Battodo*, pp. 69, 196.
15. A *shinsakutō* that has not been shortened.
16. Of course, the result will change a little if we use a *dōbari* or a *kotō*, but it is only a matter of a few cm and does not matter here.
17. What we call the "official" *monouchi*.
18. *Dictionary of Kendo* (1996), p. 72; *Dictionary of Kendo* (2000), p. 65; *Dictionary of Kendo* (2011), p. 70.

Bibliography

AJKF, *Japanese-English Dictionary of Kendo*, first edition, Tokyo, 1996.
AJKF, *Japanese-English Dictionary of Kendo*, second edition, Tokyo, 2000.
AJKF, *Japanese-English Dictionary of Kendo*, third edition, Tokyo, 2011.
AJKF, *Nippon Kendo Kata, Instruction Manual*, Tokyo, 2002.
IKF, *The Regulations of Kendo Shiai and Shinpan, The Subsidiary Rules of Kendo Shiai and Shinpan, The Guidelines for Kendo Shiai and Shinpan*, Revised July 24, 1996, Tokyo, 1996.
IKF, *The Regulations of Kendo Shiai and Shinpan, The Subsidiary Rules of Kendo Shiai and Shinpan, The Guidelines for Kendo Shiai and Shinpan*, Revised December 7, 2006, Tokyo, 2006.
Cross, R. *Physics of Baseball & Softball*, New York, 2011.
Latham, J. "The Shape of Sword Blades", in *Journal of the Royal United Service Institution*, 6, 1863, pp. 410-422.
Nakamura, T. *The Spirit of the Sword, Iaido, Kendo, and Test Cutting with the Japanese Sword*, Berkeley, 2013.
Reniez, J.-P. *Le Battodo ou la voie authentique du sabre japonais*, Luisant, 1999.
Turner, G.L. *Dynamics of Hand-Held Impact Weapons*, 2002.

Does the Time of the Attacking Action in Kendo Influence the Success Rate of Ippon?

By James Gordon Ogle

ABSTRACT

The aim of this study was to investigate whether the time of an attacking action influences the success rate of *ippon* (valid point) in international, elite level kendo matches. There is a lack of variability analysis in the area of performance and technique to find an optimum range for performance timings. This gives rise to the question of whether or not successful elite level kendo athletes are able to reproduce successful movements better than their unsuccessful counterparts.

CHAPTER I: INTRODUCTION

Many books and articles have been published on kendo which look at technique, and its basic principles (Budden, 2000; Craig, 1999; Donohue, 1999; Ozawa, 1997; Sasamori and Warner, 1964 and Tokeshi, 2003). There is however a noticeable lack of literature based upon competition performance.

1.1 Scope

This investigation will focus on elite level international kendo. A range of subjects will be analysed using the available video footage for the European and World Kendo Championships. Competitors will only be analysed if they have reached the last 16 of the individuals' tournament or higher, as this will eliminate any comparatively low-level fighters from the analysis, and will allow a more accurate reflection of whether or not there is an optimal range of attack timing in international level competitive kendo.

1.2 Hypotheses

H0a – There will be no specific range of timings that produce *ippon*.

H1a – The success rate of *ippon* will differ between strikes of differing speeds.

H0b – There will be no difference in the range of timings between all levels of the competition measured.

H1b – The competitors in the final and semifinal matches will show a more consistent range of timings than those in the last 16 and quarter finals.

CHAPTER II: LITERATURE REVIEW

2.1 Kendo Literature

The aim of this investigation is to see whether a shorter striking time in elite level kendo affects the success rate of *ippon*, and whether or not there is an optimal range of striking time that would produce *ippon* more often. This section will review the literature currently available on kendo and the areas covered. This is necessary before considering technique and biomechanics through video analysis. Finally timing analysis and factors influencing performance will be reviewed as the striking action and scoring of *ippon* depends not just on the speed and technique of the attacking competitor, but also on what the other fighter does in response.

Papers by Hukumoto (1976) and Ueda (1985) both investigate the coordination between arm and leg movement during striking in kendo. This coordination when striking is defined as *ki-ken-tai-itchi* (spirit, sword and body as one) in which synchronisation of body, mind and technique is required for the strike to be deemed valid. Miyamoto and Yamagami (1997) investigated the relationship between the weight of the *shinai* and cutting movement. Of particular interest is Tsuboi and Imai's (1986) investigation of cutting speed as an indicator of successful strikes in kendo. However, only the titles of these papers are available in English. The subject matter of these papers, availability, and lack of follow up studies in English are factors in the reason for this study and some of its protocols.

A commonly examined area in kendo, and in most martial arts, is the subject of health and safety. Saito (2006) looked at the occurrence of hypothermia in kendo and found that there were five cases of hypothermia that resulted in death among kendo practitioners between 1975 and 1997. He also suggests understanding the necessity of more frequent breaks for rehydration when training in hot weather and full kendo armour is also lacking in Japan. Nakiri et. al (2005) investigated the safety of the kendo headgear (*men*) in protecting the head from damage when receiving a *men* strike. Nakiri found that a *men* attack has a low possibility of damage, and that a single impact is not enough to cause lasting damage; however, further research is needed to investigate the effects of continuous or long-term impacts. Honda and Sumi (1997) also investigated the relationship between impact force and the striking movement in kendo. They looked at several variations of *men* strikes. These included a fundamental form where the *shinai* followed a large arcing movement before impact, a small fast cut where the *shinai* followed the shortest route to its target, and a strike where the *shinai* was raised to a vertical position and then pushed forward towards the target (which beginners commonly do). The final cut they analysed was very similar to the small fast cut. The authors specify that the measurement was taken during training to gather results from strikes during actual fighting. They found that large cuts produced the highest vertical force (presented as Mean ± Standard Deviation (204.43 ± 63.78 kgw)), and small cuts produced the lowest force (99.48 ± 37.37 kgw).

Nakiri (2006) examines the development of safe kendo training equipment by looking at both the *shinai* and *bōgu*, and looked at how the weight of the *shinai* was regulated, and how the length of the leather cap at the point was also increased to 50mm to provide added support to the *shinai* tip. The circumferences of the sixth and seventh bars from the top of the *men* were increased by 0.5 mm in order to strengthen them, and the space between these bars was increased to 15 mm. These were some of the regulations introduced to improve the safety of *shinai* and *bōgu*. Due to past accidents and fatalities resulting from kendo practice, Nakiri concluded that research is urgently needed to find ways of making training equipment safer.

One of the most common types of injury in kendo are foot injuries, and they are not restricted to any particular age, gender or experience level. A young male kendoka reported foot pain, as shown by Sakamoto et al. (1989), and was diagnosed with a stress fracture of

the medial malleolus. Okada et al. (1995) reported an occurrence of osteoid osteoma in the fifth metatarsal of another young kendoka. Nunn et al. (1997) investigated foot pain experienced in elite level female kendoka. The results showed four out of the five subjects were suffering from plantar fasciitis.

A variety of books and articles have been published describing what kendo is, its history, and what is required from a technical perspective. Some articles have looked at technique in kendo and its basic principles, but very few (and none in English) have compared technique between different grades in kendo to ascertain where the difference lies in terms of advancement through training and time.

2.2 Analysis of Technique

The term *technique* is often used but rarely defined. The Dictionary of Sport Science (1992) describes technique as a specific sequence of movements, or parts of a movement, used in solving movement tasks in sporting situations. Technique can also be defined as "the pattern and sequence of movements" (Carr, 1997: p5). Technique analysis is used to understand the way in which sports skills are performed, and therefore provide the basis for improved performance. It is used primarily within the teaching and coaching of sports skills, and also in the field of sports biomechanics (Lees, 2002).

Biomechanics is the study of motion, and its causes in living organisms. It provides mathematical and conceptual information that is necessary for understanding

how living things move (Knudson, 2007), and how they interact with the environment around them (Robertson et al., 2004).

Biomechanics is a branch of kinesiology, literally translated as "the study of movement" (Knudson, 2007: p3). Biomechanics is then broken down into two more subdivisions of kinematics and kinetics. Kinematics is concerned with the quantities that describe motion, such as acceleration, displacement and distance; whereas kinetics is concerned with the forces that result from or cause the motion of bodies (Grimshaw et al., 2006).

Motion analysis is the science of comparing images captured from photographing a body in action to study the kinematics and kinetics involved. It can be used to test the action of prosthetic devices, determine the evolution of movement patterns, and most importantly in the context of this study, to develop more efficient training programmes for athletes. Motion analysis can be split into three categories which are 2D motion analysis, 3D motion analysis, and force and pressure measurement (Griffiths, 2006).

According to Griffiths, 2D analysis using digital video cameras is a low-cost and convenient way to capture images of relatively large objects in movement. Almost all analysis is now done with computer software such as Quintic Biomechanics which maps the images for detailed investigation.

2.3 Video Analysis

Research in video or motion analysis is varied and wide ranging. Available literature has investigated the susceptibility or likelihood of injury from specific movements, to ascertain the effectiveness of video analysis in screening for injuries, and for describing technique as a visual learning aid. For example, McLean et al. (2005) investigated the likelihood of anterior cruciate ligament injury in basketball players. They quantified 20 National Collegiate Athletic Association basketball players using 3D knee valgus and 2D frontal plane knee angle during side step, side jump, and shuttle run tasks using external marker coordinates, frontal plane projections and manual digitisation of digital video footage. They found that the 2D method can be used to screen for excessive valgus, particularly for movements occurring primarily in the frontal plane.

Hazen et al. (1990) investigated video feedback results on helping improve performance in youth swimmers. They found the video feedback package they used to be effective in improving performance in different strokes. Nicholls et al. (2003) found 2D motion analysis using video recording equipment to have low sensitivity when filming baseball pitching. However, this only seems to be a problem with extremely rapid movements or actions, i.e. the arm acceleration phase lasting only 0.15s (Dillman et al., 1993–cited in Nicholls et al., 2003) in baseball pitching.

Gribble et al. (2005) investigated the reliability and validity of kinematic analysis through digitisation of video from a single camera, with subjects carrying out a star excursion balance test. They found that the 2D camera system offers a low-cost system for reporting single-plane kinematics with strong reliability and reasonable validity.

Mannon et al. (1997) compared video-based motion analysis and electromagnetic motion analysis measurement of 2D rear foot motion during walking. Their results show no significant difference between the results produced by the two types of analysis. Due to the nature of the clear start and end point for attacks in kendo, video analysis would be most appropriate as the action can be measured from wherever the camera has been set up as long as the video quality is adequate.

According to the results of Mannon et al. (1997), the use of video analysis instead of electromagnetic motion analysis will not affect the results of a study, although the electromagnetic method may be much faster for analysis than the video analysis method. There is, however, no specification of the type of electromagnetic motion analysis equipment, and no follow up studies by the authors involving its use. This lack of specification and literature involving electromagnetic motion analysis suggests a lack of support or interest in replacing 2-D motion analysis.

There seems to be no disadvantage in using video software to enhance or improve performance, even though it is by far the slower method compared to electromagnetic testing according to Mannon et al. (1997) .

2.4. Timing Analysis

A number of papers (Barrentine et al., 1998; Elliott et al., 1988; Pinto Neto et al., 2007; Seifert and Chollet, 2005 and Stodden et al., 2005) have used video analysis to investigate temporal factors. Much of the data on temporal analysis investigates throwing technique or pitching in baseball. For example, Elliott et al. (1988) used temporal data synchronised with kinematic data to find peak ground reaction forces at different intervals of the action in baseball pitching. They found that mean forces produced were similar for the three fastest pitchers when compared to the three slowest pitchers, and that the slower group produced their peak force earlier in the pitching action, thus reducing their ability to drive over a stabilised front leg.

Seifert and Chollet (2005) examined arm and leg coordination during flat breaststroke in nine male and eight female elite swimmers. Coordination was expressed using temporal gaps which described the continuity between the propulsive phases of the limbs recorded on a video device (50 Hz). Expertise in the flat breaststroke was characterised by synchronised arm and leg recoveries and continuity in arm and leg propulsions with increasing velocity. Differences between the genders in the spatio-temporal parameters were possibly due to anthropometric differences, and different motor organisation linked to arm and leg coordination. They conclude that temporal gap measurement and the index of flat breaststroke propulsion are indicators of arm and leg coordination. This can be exploited by coaches and swimmers to improve the continuity between propulsive actions during the flat breaststroke.

Pinto Neto et al., (2007) investigated hand speed in Kung-fu practitioners compared to non-practitioners when striking a ball. Hand and ball speed were determined by high-speed video analysis. Their results showed that kung fu practitioners have a higher hand speed than non-practitioners, and suggest that for impacts against heavier objects, the effective mass would be the main factor to distinguish between a martial artist and an untrained subject. This difference in hand speed between practitioners and non-practitioners relates well to the duration of attacks in kendo at the elite level and whether or not this can affect the success rate of *ippon*.

Barrentine et al. (1998) and Stodden et al. (2005) both investigated throwing mechanics in baseball pitching. Barrentine et al. (1998) looked at kinematic data of the wrist and forearm in three different types of throw in baseball, and found fast and curve ball pitching to show the highest peak wrist extension. Stodden et al. (2005) examined the effects of seven kinetic, 11 temporal,

and 12 kinematic parameters on pitched ball velocity. They found that three kinetic parameters, two temporal parameters and three kinematic parameters were significantly related to increased ball velocity. They suggest that pitchers should focus on consistent mechanics to produce consistently high fastball velocities. This consistency of technique suggested by Stodden et al. (2005) also relates to this investigation, as the question of striking speed being the major contributor to scoring *ippon* is often raised at national team camps between competitive kendoka. Such knowledge could help dictate whether competitors need to be faster to be better, or if they should focus more on the timing and pressure aspects of their kendo earlier in their competitive careers, and not just on quicker movements.

Vodicar and Jost (2011) investigated kinematic parameters in ski-jumping. Of particular relevance was their recording of "time of flying" between the best, average, and below average jumpers. This measurement of "time of flying" is akin to the "time of the attacking action" to be recorded in this investigation. Vodicar and Jost (2011) focused primarily on other kinematic parameters, such as in-run velocity, out-run velocity and vertical height of flying. Vodicar and Jost used a correlation analysis and single factor ANOVA to analyse their results, and found that the ski jumpers with the highest vertical height in their flight curve achieved the best jumps with p values of <0.01.

As previously stated, this investigation will incorporate various methods used in research in other sporting disciplines, and aims to show whether the time of an attack affects its success rate. The main population to benefit from this investigation is the kendoka outside of Japan and Korea. However, the concept of an optimum range for performance variables is applicable across many (if not all) sports.

2.5 Concept of advantage / Factors influencing performance—athlete quality or level

The concept of 'home advantage' is often discussed and investigated in sports literature. Courneya and Carron (1992) describe the phenomenon that home teams in sporting competitions win more than 50% of their matches in a balanced home and away schedule. Although this investigation is not looking at whether or not there is a home advantage in kendo competition, it could provide another insight into the area of external factors affecting performance. For example, it is plausible that technical aspects (in this case, "time of attack") are affected by a particular opponent from countries (such as Japan or Korea) who are widely believed to be faster or better because of their countries prior performances and reputation.

Marcelino et al., (2011) looked into the effects of match status and opponent quality on technical and tactical performance in volleyball. They used a multinominal logistic regression to evaluate the relationship between match status and tactical indicators with a statistical significance set at p <0.05. They found that unbalanced matches in terms of team quality resulted in more risky tactical decisions. More evenly balanced matches involved less risk taking regardless of whether one team had the advantage in that particular match. According to Marcelino, their research was contrary to previous findings (Eom and Schutz, (1992) and Taylor et al., (2008)) regarding technical variables being affected by situational variables in both volleyball and football. They attribute this to the level of the players. High level players consistently reveal high technical proficiency, and success at this level is mainly dependant on tactical performance (Hughes and Bartlett, 2002).

Due to the nature of kendo, these findings are of particular interest, and provide a good basis for further investigation into whether the technical aspects (time of the attacking movement) or tactical aspects (whether or not a specific opponent or team cause a change in the time of the attacking movements successfully) are the most beneficial for performance at international level.

2.6 *Summary of Findings*
The current research and information available in English is very limited, particularly in terms of understanding the timing of movements, timing outcome in kendo, and anything involving the concept of optimal timing in relation to competition success.

Optimal timing and range is an area that needs much more study across all sports, and using kendo as an example of whether or not a successful outcome can be achieved if specific factors are within this optimal range, could benefit athletes of all levels in a diverse range of sports.

CHAPTER III: METHODS

3.1 *Analysis of Variability*
Previous works (Andrews et al., 2011; Durovic et al., 2008; Hiley and Yeadon, 2003; Loturco et al., 2013; Tran and Silverberg, 2008) have looked at differences in means and the statistical representation of these differences through measures of dispersion. Others have investigated the application of statistical approaches to reduce the inter-subject variation (Montelpare et al., 2013). Of particular interest is Gregson et al., (2010) who investigated the variability of distances covered in "high-speed activities" (total high speed running distance, high speed running, total spring distance and total number of sprints undertaken) in Premier League football.

Gregson et al., (2010) concluded that football players do not reproduce high-speed activity profiles across different games over a period of time due to weather affects, possession, and position of play. Although these particular affects are not applicable to kendo, the situation of being in a winning position (having a one point lead over the opponent) and exerting an effect on the speed of actions is. The basis of the investigation by Gregson et al. follows the same area of variability in elite sporting levels and although they may look at the variability in performance for elite level athletes and it was found that match to match variability of these elite athletes is very high, all actions that were <0.5s in length were not included, whereas in kendo many of the attacking actions occur in <0.2s.

However, there is a lack of statistical analysis studying timing variability itself, and comparing different standard deviations in regards to the ability to reproduce a higher performance. This lack of variability analysis in the area of performance and technique analysis to find an optimum range for performance timings gives rise to the following question: are successful elite athletes able to reproduce successful movements better than their unsuccessful counterparts based on timing and speed variability? The analysis of variability will provide a deeper understanding of optimal performance and technique, especially in sports where the outcome of technique does not rely on the concept of "faster (or more) is better". This concept indicates that a high variability means that the athlete is unable to consistently produce the optimal level of performance or technique. In sports where speed is not the most important factor, or where more is not necessarily better, a higher level of variability at the elite level could display an athlete's ability to change technique to suit the current situation of the match or bout.

3.2 Study Design

The selected videos were viewed using Kinovea where the time of the attacking action could be viewed frame by frame. Due to the video quality, the time between each frame differed slightly (from 0.01s to 0.02s). The video was paused each time an attack was made by either competitor and the attacking movement was measured and timed using the synchronised stopwatch in Kinovea and noted down in Microsoft Excel 2010. Each movement was measured from the start of the forward or downward movement of the *shinai* until the point of impact with the target, the opponents' *shinai* if they blocked, a non-valid target area, or until the point of the *shinai* had passed through the target area if the cut was a complete miss. The aim was to look at the proportion of different outcomes for attacks of different time durations. The variability in times between conditions was compared as well as mean timings.

3.3 Apparatus

The data was analysed using Kinovea 0.8.15, Microsoft Excel 2010 and SPSS 14.0 for Windows (SPSS, SPSS: An IBM Company, Amarouk, NY: USA).

3.4 Data

Video footage was taken from international *taikai* (competitions) where all participants were selected by their home nation to be an international representative (World Kendo Championships, European Kendo Championships, 5 Nations Kendo Championships). Matches where the recording equipment or viewpoint were unable to capture the point of impact for strikes were excluded, and the videos used were only selected from the men's individual matches from the last 16 through to the final. The rounds before the last 16 were omitted so that only the elite level were analysed. The rationale for this was that many countries with national teams who are less experienced, or only newly formed, will not perform at the same level as other well established teams. Therefore their cutting and movement time would not be an accurate representation of elite level performance and many fights from the first rounds of competition are not recorded or available. Selection of videos was dependant on public availability on the internet as many videos of finalists that are recorded by their teammates are kept privately for team analysis. The videos that are in the public domain are either those provided by the event organisers and promotional team, or recorded by spectators at the event.

3.5 Data analysis

Each cutting action from the start of the downward or forward motion to the point of impact (See figure 1) was measured and recorded as one of the following outcomes:

Ippon——— if the point was awarded
1 flag ——— if one referee awarded the point but the other two disagreed
Hit ——— if the cut hit the target but no referee awarded the point
Blocked– if the cut was stopped from hitting the target by the opponents body or shinai
Missed—— if the cut landed away from a target area or missed the opponent completely

The duration of the attacking time was recorded under the relevant outcome in Excel for each attack in each *taikai*, and also for the winner and loser of each match. The results were grouped into separate competitions for ease of recording, and then copied onto a "Total" sheet where the measurements were separated into outcome of strike for winner and loser in the top-16, quarterfinals, semifinals, and finals. The mean and SD were calculated for each round, and for the total values for each variable as well as for the total winners and losers.

This is not a direct matched comparison between winning and losing kendo competitors as competitors do not always perform the same number of strikes. Therefore,

Start of forward/downward motion   *Point of impact with target*

Figure 1. Striking action for an attack that results in Ippon.

a paired samples t-test would not be possible. Instead, independent samples t-tests were used to compare the timings of strikes performed by the winners and losers of each match.

There are five classes of strike outcome. Not all performances involved all classes of outcome. Some involved multiple occurrences of the same outcome type. Therefore, a one-way ANOVA was used to compare timings of strikes leading to different outcomes, along with round of the competition and the level of success or final round reached by the fighter rather than a repeated measure ANOVA.

Levene's tests were then carried out to compare the variability in timings between athletes, the separate rounds of the competitions, the final round reached, and also for the outcome of the attacks. The Levene's tests were most important to find if an optimal range was present in each of these areas as it is an inferential statistic used to assess the equality of variances for a variable calculated for two or more groups.

CHAPTER IV: RESULTS

4.1 Frequency of attacking time

Figure 2 demonstrates the attacking time (grouped into brackets of 0.03s or 0.04s) for each attack made by the winners and losers of each match analysed. The winners of the matches present a noticeably higher frequency of attacks between 0.09s and 0.12s and attacks with a duration of ≥0.24s. Although the SD between the two groups shown in Table 1 shows a noticeable margin, Levene's test shows the difference not to be significant at p=0.26.

4.2 Time of attack in relation to the outcome

The chi square test does not show the proportionate breakdowns to be significantly different between the timing groups (X^2_{20} = 25.2, p = 0.194) but Table 2 shows that 7.6% of 0.09-0.12s attempts and 6.5% of 0.13-0.15s attempts lead to *ippon* – these are higher proportions than other timing zones, as shown by Figure 3, suggesting there is an optimal speed that increases the chance of *ippon*.

For the time of attack in relation to the outcome, both Levene's test (p=0.22) and ANOVA test (p=0.29) presented a non-significant result even though the *ippon* outcome shows a clearly lower mean and SD.

4.3 Attacking time per round of the competition

Though Figure 4 shows the SD for the last 16 is more than double that of the other rounds, Levene's test showed the difference not to be significant (p=0.49) and the ANOVA test also showed a non-significant value of p=0.2

4.4 Attack times for the final round reached

Levene's test and an ANOVA test both presented significance values of p=<0.01 and a Bonferroni correction also a significance value of p<0.01 when comparing the last 16 with the semifinals and finals. The Bonferroni results for the last 16 and quarterfinals (p=0.07) as well as the quarterfinals against the semifinals and finals (p=1.00) were not significant.

Table 1. Mean and Standard Deviation of Attacking Time between Winners and Losers

Match Outcome	Mean	SD
Winners	0.14s	0.05s
Losers	0.16s	0.11s

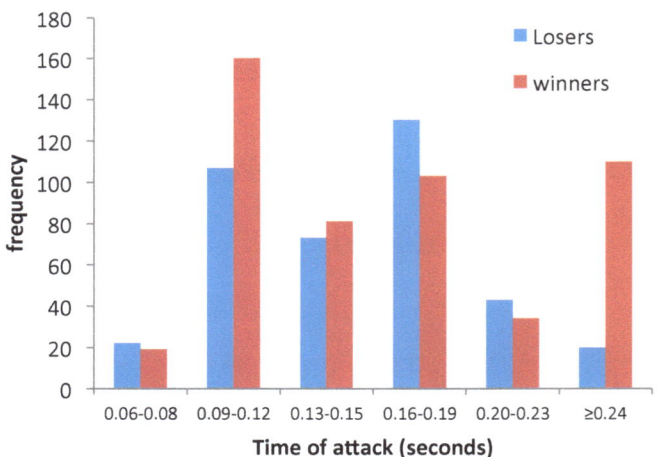

Figure 2. Frequency of attacking time

Table 2. Percentage of Total Attacks that Lead to *Ippon* in Each Timing Group

Time	<=0.08s	0.09-0.12s	0.13-0.15s	0.16-0.19s	0.20-0.23s	>=0.24s
%	4.88	7.57	6.49	2.15	2.6	0

CHAPTER V: DISCUSSION

The aim of this study was to investigate whether or not the time of an attacking action influenced the success rate of *ippon* in international level kendo. The main findings of the study show that all the variables investigated, apart from one (attack times for the final round reached by the individual), presented non-significant differences in SD, but still showed a clear margin in the SD and produced noticeable differences between them.

These results show that the shortest attacking times, or the fastest attacks, do not always result in *ippon* being scored. However, the attacks that took 0.24s or longer did not result in any *ippon* being scored at all. This suggests that there is an optimal timing range in kendo that produces a winning strike.

Within this study, data collection was a limiting factor due to video availability. As the videos were viewed from a public domain, their availability was dependant on other people around the world uploading them, and making them publicly accessible. It also meant that not all fights from certain competitions were available, as some people will only film fighters from their own country or from the semifinals and finals. The number of videos found of good enough quality to analyse was enough to give an adequate pool of data to investigate, but more videos of complete competitions filmed for the purpose of analysis instead of from an individual's hand-held mobile device would render more accurate results.

5.1 Pre-Analysis Expectations

Before data collection began, two hypotheses were made based on the study design and available literature: 1. The success rate of *ippon* would differ between strikes of differing speeds; 2. Competitors in the final and semifinal matches would show a more consistent range of timings than those in the last 16 and quarterfinals. These were based upon findings such as those by Stodden et al. (2005), who suggested that baseball pitchers should focus on consistent mechanics to produce the highest pitching speeds. These consistent mechanics allow the athlete to produce their optimum performance, speed, and action for longer, and produce it when required rather than intermittently. For kendo, this means that the consistent range of times which would be the optimum will be

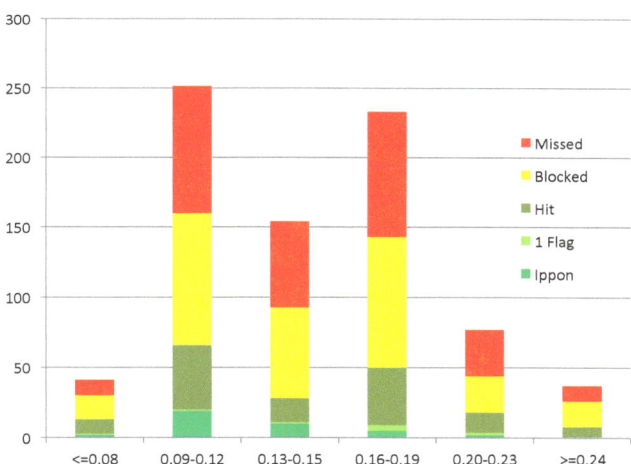

Figure 3. Number of outcomes per time zone

Table 3. Mean and SD for the Time of Attack in Relation to the Outcome

Outcome	Mean	SD
Missed	0.15s	0.05s
Blocked	0.16s	0.12s
Hit	0.15s	0.05s
1 Flag	0.17s	0.07s
Ippon	0.13s	0.03s

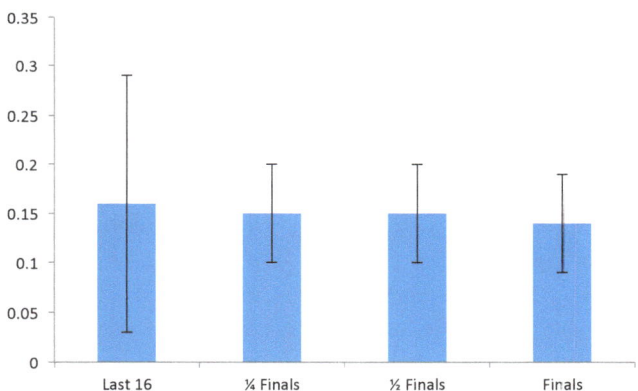

Figure 4. Mean and SD for attacking time per competition round

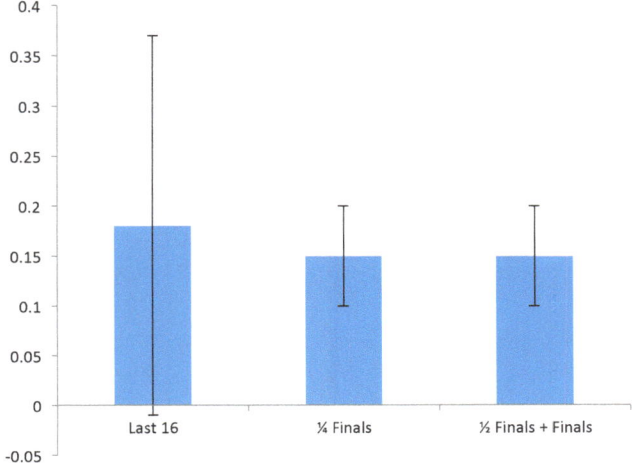

Figure 5. Attack times for the final round reached by the individual

produced by the most elite athletes, which will then manifest in the later rounds showing a more consistent range.

5.2. Timing of Strikes and Outcome
The successful athletes were faster. The optimal time of attack for success suggests that if an attack was too slow, then it was easily dodged or blocked. If it was too fast, then the attack did not have the accuracy required to score the point.

Winners of matches also present a noticeably higher frequency of attacks between 0.09s and 0.12s, a slightly higher frequency of attacks between 0.13s and 0.15s, and also a much higher frequency of attacks with a duration of ≥0.24s.

The increased frequency of attacks between 0.09s and 0.15s for the winners of the matches links well with the fact that the highest number of *ippon* are scored within this time range. The overall mean time of attack is 0.02s faster in the winning athletes, and only has an SD of 0.05s which is much lower than the losing SD of 0.11s.

When we look at the outcomes of the attacks, the mean time resulting in *ippon* is the lowest of all the outcomes at 0.13s, and also has the lowest SD of 0.03. This range of 0.10s to 0.16s would be the optimal range, and fits very closely with the highest frequency of *ippon* in the data groups 0.09s to 0.15s. The higher consistency of shorter attacking times produced by the winners may be explained by the work of Pinto Neto et al., (2007), in which martial-arts trained practitioners exhibited higher hand speed during striking. Though the difference in this investigation is not between trained and untrained, the level between the winners and losers can reflect a difference in years of training or experience.

The only unexpected figure from the frequency of attacking time is the much higher frequency of ≥0.24s attacks for the winners. This could be due to a number of different factors; the two most likely being a tactical manoeuvre to change their cutting time so that the opponent is thrown off guard, or taken by surprise or the use of *renzoku-waza* or repeated attacks. These attacks take longer to execute in terms of time as they require multiple actions in the same attacking movement, but can be used to change the pace or position of a bout. However, none of the attacks of ≥0.24s resulted in *ippon* being scored.

5.3. Variability in Timings and Performance Level
The Levene's tests and ANOVA tests were all nonsignificant for frequency of attacking time (p=0.26), time of attack in relation to the outcome (p=0.22 and p=0.29) and attacking time per round of the competition (p=0.49 and p=0.2).

Even though these results lacked a significant level of variability, the frequency of attacking time showed a clear difference in SD, more than double for the losers of the matches and the range of SD between the timing of attacks for the different outcomes showed *ippon* to clearly have the lowest mean, and SD with 1 flag and blocked attacks having the highest. This increased variation in blocked attacks and attacks that result in 1 flag could be due to tactical processes performed by the participants. If they were to execute some slower or larger strikes that cause their opponent to react differently, or expect a certain type of action, they could then surprise them with the attack that follows which is within the optimal range. Or it could simply be due to the fact that *ippon* are scored much more often within this smaller optimal range, and the individuals who are knocked out in the last 16 are performing larger actions that take a longer time, and are therefore not performing within the optimal range.

When the attack times for the final round reached by the individual were investigated and the last 16 were compared with the semifinals and finals, Levene's test and the ANOVA test both presented highly significant values (p<0.01).

Grouping the semifinals and finals together this way was done with the reasoning that those that have reached the semifinals are usually performing at the same level as the finalists, and this level of the competition is often a very close result where the winner could be either competitor. Thus, the variability in the actions is lower as the top individuals are consistently producing their optimal range.

The significance level of the Levene's test and ANOVA test between these groups shows that the level being demonstrated even in the last 16 of elite level competitions is still highly variable. The SD in the last 16 group is again more than double that of the other groups. This suggests that, even though 50% of the competitors in the last 16 progress to the quarterfinals, those that do not are showing a much higher variation in their attacking times. It is only when we reach the quarterfinals that the bouts become more even in terms of attacking time and repeatability.

This higher variability shown by the last 16 follows the trend found by Seifert and Chollet (2005) in the semifinalists and finalists in elite swimming events. This indicates better "continuity" or a lower variability in their attacking actions. The same study also found that the swimmers that produced the best times were also showing a shorter recovery phase between actions. Therefore, the forward propulsion was more effective, which is much like the shorter striking times with less superfluous movement produced by the finalists.

Performing within this optimal range will allow the competitors to produce striking actions in elite level kendo that are fast enough to be effective but also have enough accuracy to be awarded as *ippon*. Training and performing within this optimal range will therefore facilitate a much more productive movement that would result in more strikes being effective and therefore more likely to score *ippon*.

5.4 Approaches to Interpreting Performance Indicators

Mean and SD across all the results showed a clear difference between winners and losers, and for scoring *ippon*. The sample size gave almost exactly the same total number of attacks for both winners and losers (398 and 395 respectively), so the analysis was not affected in terms of number of measurements when using the two groups.

Competitive success can be described as the place an individual finishes in a tournament (the final round reached), usually because the more successful can produce their optimal performance consistently. Previous research has looked at the difference between winners and losers, but this does not work when both performers are at the highest level, as they are producing results that can be very similar. This indicates that the level of each athlete must be considered.

These results have shown that successful athletes at the highest level of performance are producing faster movements and actions than those less successful or at a lower level. In other words, the most successful athletes have a higher or faster optimal range than their less successful counterparts. This implies that elite level performers should focus on making the range of times for their actions faster and more consistent.

Research into the area of changes in optimal range would give teams and coaches a model of training to build towards or maintain. Knowing if the optimal range for producing *ippon* has changed over the years, whether it has become faster or slower, would give an idea of where the sport is heading in terms of development, and what coaches can focus on to keep at the top level of performance. If the optimum range has not changed, then more work can be put into replicating this range for winning performances.

Another limitation is the reaction time of the referees, and observable actions of the competitors. As the speed of the competitor increases, the need (or calls) for external technological judging aids, such as video replay akin to those used in cricket, would become more prevalent.

However, the question remains as to whether or not speed is enough in sports or martial arts where the scoring of a point is not purely reliant on hitting the opponent before they hit you.

Using the results of this investigation, a marking scheme could be created for assessing the performance of an athlete, and seeing how close they perform to the optimum range in their training or competition. Using the results from the time of the attacks in relation to the outcome the point scheme can be based on the percentage of *ippon* scored in each time bracket (Table 4).

Based on this marking scheme, one individual kendoka who was selected to be the "gold standard" test subject for this investigation scored the results depicted in Table 5 using this system. The immediate issue that arises with this form of marking scheme, however, is that instead of just giving a higher point total for someone who does the most attacks within the optimum range, it could also give the same score to someone who does more attacks that are outside this range.

So, within a performance we would need the spread of values, not just the mean to mark variability outside the optimal range. Another way of addressing the issue of the scores inaccurately reflecting the performance would be to dimensionalise the marks based on the duration of the bout or the number of attacks made. Using the duration of the bout is reflected by information presented by O'Donoghue (2014), who showed that in elite male competitive tennis, Ivanisevic scored more aces at the Wimbledon championships than Sampras. However, Sampras was usually winning his matches in three sets, whereas Ivanisevic was taking up to four or five sets before he defeated his opponent, therefore giving him more opportunities to serve an ace. Using the number of attacks to make the scores proportionate would mean that an individual who makes 1,000 attacks but only scores two points would not end up at the same score as someone who makes 250 attacks and scores eight points. The scoring could be used to calculate how many attacks per 100 were within the optimal range or how many were of a particular duration within this bracket.

The methods utilised in this investigation, coupled with access to a performance analyst and the right software, allow for a level of feedback and information that can be used by elite level coaches and athletes throughout their training regimes and at competitions. Specifically for martial arts such as kendo, and other sports that do not have a professional aspect (at least in some countries), finding an effective and economically viable way of providing this support may be problematic. Further development of the marking scheme into an easy

Table 4. Marking scheme for Performance Assessment

Time	<=0.08s	0.09-0.12s	0.13-0.15s	0.16-0.19s	0.20-0.23s	>=0.24s
%	4.88	7.57	6.49	2.15	2.6	0
Points	5	8	7	2	3	0

to use smartphone application that can be used with any video analysis software and edited or adapted to any sport would allow all levels of participation to benefit.

CHAPTER VI: CONCLUSION

Though the shortest attacking times, or the fastest attacks, do not always result in *ippon* being scored, attacks that take 0.24s or longer do not result in any *ippon* being scored at all. This suggests that at the elite level there is a point where an attack can be too slow and will not result in successful *ippon*. Winners of matches also produced a higher frequency of attacks between 0.09s and 0.12s, a slightly higher frequency of attacks between 0.13s and 0.15s and also a much higher frequency of attacks with a duration of ≥0.24s.

The concept of an optimal range within sporting performance is present; it is the ability to reproduce this optimal range consistently that currently separates the elite level athletes from those below them. Achieving a higher ability to reproduce the optimal range will improve the level of national kendo teams around the world.

Investigations into which aspects of kendo technique have the largest effect on cutting time and/or accuracy of the cut would allow coaches and national teams to develop their skills to improve this ability to reproduce this optimum timing range for scoring *ippon*. Portus (2000) found that counter-rotation of the body in cricket fast bowling reduced the accuracy of the bowl, especially later in the bowling spell. This effect of rotation on accuracy is directly applicable to kendo as an important part of scoring *ippon* is the requirement of an upright and straight posture. I found significant differences in basic movements in a strike performed by *dan* and *kyū* grades in a laboratory setting, but further investigation is needed into the technical aspects that cause these differences to allow further improvement of an individual's performance and progression in the martial art.

Differences in cutting time and optimal range between male and female kendoka would be very valuable to the development of both the martial art as a whole, and also for future research into gender differences for elite

Table 5. Score per Match for the "Gold Standard" Athlete

Match 1	52
Match 2	82
Match 3	132
Match 4	37
Match 5	85
Match 6	57

level athletes across all sports.

Another area of interest for future research would be whether there is a smaller optimal range found at the highest level between athletes performing within what is currently considered optimal. As this investigation found the optimum range to be between 0.10s and 0.16s, further research into whether or not there is a smaller optimum range for the time of the attacking action would be beneficial. This work could also consider not just whether the attack was awarded as *ippon*, but also the quality of the strike, etc.

With optimal values, as well as variables where higher or lower values are better, an interesting question is how much weight should each variable contribute to an overall performance mark? The relative importance of different aspects needs to be considered so that the marking scheme can be both effective and applicable. This will allow the scheme to be tailored for any future changes in optimal range as well as cross-discipline use in other sports and activities. If the scheme was tested with other sports and variables, such as first serves in tennis, this would allow the marking scheme to be refined and used in all sports and disciplines and not just in kendo and the martial arts.

REFERENCES

- Andrews, C., Bakewell, J. and Scurr, J.C. (2011). Comparison of advanced and intermediate 200-m backstroke swimmers' dominant and non-dominant shoulder entry angles across various swimming speeds. *Journal of Sports Sciences*, 29(7), 743–748
- Barrentine, S.W., Matsuo, T., Escamilla, R.F., Fleisig, G.S. and Andrews, J.R. (1998). Kinematic Analysis of the Wrist and Forearm During Baseball Pitching. *Journal of Applied Biomechanics*, 14, 24–39
- Bartlett, R. (1999). *Sports Biomechanics: Reducing Injury and Improving Performance*. London: E & FN Spon. (Cited in Lees, 2002).
- Budden, P. (2000). *Looking at a Far Mountain*. USA: Tuttle Publishing
- Carr, G. (1997). *Mechanics of Sport*. Champaign, IL: Human Kinetics.
- Cometti, G., Maffiuletti, N.A., Pousson, M., Chatard, J.C. and Maffulli, N. (2001). Isokinetic Strength and Anaerobic Power of Elite, Subelite and Amateur French Soccer Players. *International Journal of Sports Medicine*, 22, 45–51.
- Courneya, K.S and Carron, A.V. (1992). The home advantage in sport competitions: A literature review. *Journal of Sport and Exercise Psychology*. 14, 13–27.
- Craig, D.M. (1999). *The Heart of Kendo*. USA: Shambhala Publishing.
- *Dictionary of Sport Science* (1992). Malaga: Unisport.
- Donohue, J. (1999). *Complete Kendo*. USA: Tuttle Publishing.
- Đurović, N., Lozovina, V., Pavičić, L. and Mrduljaš, D. (2008). Kinematic analysis of the tennis serve in young tennis players. *Acta Kinesiologica*, 2, 50–56
- Elliott, B., Grove, R. And Gibson, B. (1988). Timing of the Lower Limb Drive and Throwing Limb Movement in Baseball Pitching. *International Journal of Sports Biomechanics*, 4, 5–7
- Eom, H. and Schutz, R. (1992). Transition Play in Team Performance of Volleyball: A Log-linear Analysis. *Research Quarterly for Exercise and Sport*, 63, 261–269
- Gale, D. (1971). Optimal strategy for serving in tennis. *Mathematics Magazine*, 5, 197-9.
- Garrison, J.C., Hart, J.M., Palmieri, R.M., Kerrigan, D.C. and Ingersoll, C.D. (2005). Lower Extremity EMG in Male and Female College Soccer Players During Single-Leg Landing. *Journal of Sport Rehabilitation*, 14, 48–57
- Goodwin, M. (2012). Private communication
- Gorostiaga, E.M., Granados, C., Ibáñez, J. and Izquierdo, M. (2005). Differences in Physical Fitness and Throwing Velocity Among Elite and Amateur Male Handball Players. *International Journal of Sports Medicine*, 26, 225–232
- Gregson, W., Drust, B., Atkinson, G. and Salvo, V. D. (2010) Match-to-Match Variability of High-Speed Activities in Premier League Soccer, *Int J Sports Med 2010*; 31: 237–242
- Gribble, P., Hertel, J., Denegar, C. and Buckley, W. (2005). Reliability and Validity of a 2-DVideo Digitizing System During a Static and a Dynamic Task. *Journal of Sports Rehabilitation*, 14, 137–149
- Griffiths, I. (2006). *Principles of Biomechanics & Motion Analysis*. USA: Lippincott Williams & Wilkins.
- Grimshaw, P., Lees, A., Fowler, N. and Burden, A. (2006). *Sport & Exercise Biomechanics*. UK: Taylor & Francis Group.
- Hay, J.G. and Reid, G. (1982). *Anatomy, Mechanics and Human Motion*. Englewood Cliffs, NJ: Prentice-Hall. (Cited in Lees, 2002).
- Hazen, A., Johnstone, C., Martin, G.L. and Srikameswaran, S. (1990). A Videotaping Feedback Package for Improving Skills of Youth Competitive Swimmers. *The Sport Psychologist*, 4, 213–227
- Hiley, M.J. and Yeadon, M.R. (2003). Optimum Technique for Generating Angular Momentum in Accelerated Backward Giant Circles Prior to a Dismount. *Journal of Applied Biomechanics*, 19, 119-130
- Honda, S. and Sumi, M. (1997). *A Study on Quality of Shomen-Uchi in Kendo: On the Relationship Between Impact Force and Hitting Movement*. Masters Thesis. Fukuoka University of Education.
- Hukumoto, S. (1976). Study of hitting motion in Kendo. Coordination between arm and leg movement. [Online]. *Bulletin of the Institute of Physical Education, Keio University* 16, 71. Abstract from Ebsco Host Research Databases. Available from URL: http://web.ebscohost.com/ehost/detail?vid=4&hid=4&sid=f3dc1151-fc7e-4988-9f79-e0e50315e137%40sessionmgr7 [Cited 03-09-13].
- Kiyota, M. (2002). *The Shambhala Guide to Kendo*. USA: Shambhala Publishing.
- Knudson, D. (2007). *Fundamentals of Biomechanics*. USA: Springer Science and Business Media, LLC.
- Koda, K., Yoshitani, O., Arita, Y and Nabeyama, T. (2005). A study on constituent elements of effective strikes in kendo-Setting modern significance and viewpoints. *Bulletin of Institute of Health and Sport Sciences, University of Tsukuba (Ibaraki-ken)*, 28, 73–78
- Lees, A. (2002). *Technique Analysis in Sports: a Critical Review*. *Journal of sports sciences*, 20, 813–828
- Loturco, I., Ugrinowitsch, C., Roschel, H., Tricoli, V. and González-Badillo, J. J. (2013). Training at the Optimum Power Zone Produces Similar Performance Improvements to Traditional Strength Training. *Journal of Sports Science and Medicine*, 12, 109–115.
- Mannon, K., Anderson, T., Cheetham, P., Cornwall, M.W. and McPoil, T.G. (1997). A Comparison of *two Motion Analysis* Systems for the Measurement of *Two-Dimensional* Rear Foot *Motion* During Walking. *Foot & ankle international,* [Online]. 18, 427–431. Abstract from Ebsco Host Research Databases. Available from URL: http://search.ebscohost.com/login.aspx?direct=true&db=s3h&AN=SPH436753&site=ehost-live [Cited 23-10-13].
- Marcelino, R., Mesquita, I. and Sampaio, J. (2011). Effects

- of Quality of Opposition and Match Status on Technical and Tactical Performances in Elite Volleyball. *Journal of Sports Sciences*, 29 (7), 733–741
- Mathlin, G. (2011). Private communication
- McLean, S.G., Walker, K., Ford, K.R., Myer, G.D., Hewett, T.E., and van den Bogert, J.A. (2005). Evaluation of a two dimensional analysis method as a screening and evaluation tool for anterior cruciate ligament injury. *British Journal of Sports Medicine*, 39, 355-362
- Miyamoto, K. and Yamagami, S. (1997). A study of the relationship between the weight of shinai and striking motion in elementary school aged kendoists. *Book of abstracts, International Society of Biomechanics*, 95
- Montelpare, W., McPherson, M. and Puumala, R. (2013). Statistical Analysis of Athlete Variability Applied to Biomechanical Analysis of Ski Jumping. *International Journal of Sports Science & Coaching.* 8 (2), 373–384.
- Nakiri, F. (2006). Research into the Development of Safe Kendo Training Equipment. [Online]. Available from URL: http://www.budo.ac/kendo/kendo_archves_e/nakiri_2006/nakiri_2006.htm [Cited 15-12-13].
- Nakiri, F., Yokoyama, N., Arita, Y., Kubo, T. and Yamagami, S. (2005). Influence of Datotsu in Kendo on the Human Head: Impact Estimation Using Simulation with Crash Dummy. Research Journal of Budo, 37, 1–64
- Nicholls, R., Fleisig, G., Elliott, B., Lyman, S. and Osinski, E. (2003). Accuracy of Qualitative Analysis for Assessment of Skilled Baseball Pitching Technique. *Sports Biomechanics, 2 (2), 213–226*
- Nunn, N.R., Dyas, J.W. and Parker Dodd, I. (1997). Repetitive Strain Injury to the Foot in Elite Women Kendoka. *British Journal of Sports Medicine,* 31, 68–69
- O'Donoghue, P. (2014). Interpreting Performance Indicators with Optimal Values. Carecas, Spain, 15th November 2014, Spanish Association of Sports Sciences.
- Ogle, J.G. (2008). *The difference in technique between different grades of Kendoka: An investigation of five different aspects of technique between Dan and Kyu grades.* BSc Thesis. University of Gloucestershire.
- Okada, K., Senma, S., Abe, E. and Sato, K. (1995). Stress Fractures of the Medial Malleolus: A Case Report. *Foot and Ankle International,* 16, 49–52
- Ozawa, H. (1997). *Kendo the Definitive Guide.* UK: Kodansha International Ltd.
- Pinto Neto, O., Magini, M. and Saba, M.M.F. (2007). The Role of Effective Mass and Hand Speed in the Performance of Kung Fu Athletes Compared With Nonpractitioners. *Journal of Applied Biomechanics*, 23, 139–148
- Portus, M.R., Mason, B.R., Elliott, B.C., Pfitzner, M.c. and Done, R.P. (2000). Technique Factors Related to Ball Release Speed and Trunk Injuries in High Performance Cricket Fast Bowlers. *Sports Biomechanics*, 3, (2), 263–285.
- Robertson, G.E., Caldwell, G.E., Hamill, J., Kamen, G. and Whittlesey, S.N. (2004). *Research Methods in Biomechanics.* Leeds: Human Kinetics.
- Saito, M. (2006). Hyperthermia in Kendo. [Online]. Available from URL: http://www.budo.ac/kendo/kendo_archves_e/hyperthermia_2006/hyperthermia.htm [Cited 06-11-13].
- Sakamoto, K., Mizuta, H., Okajima, K. and Kitagawa, T. (1989). An unusual cause of metatarsal pain in a young kendo player. American Orthopaedic Society for Sports Medicine, 17, 297–297
- Sasamori, J and Warner, G. (1964). *This is Kendo*. USA: Tuttle Publishing.
- Schade, F., Arampatzis, A., Bruggemann, G.P. and Komi, P.V. (2004). Comparison of the men's and the women's pole vault at the 2000 Sydney Olympic Games. *Journal of Sports Sciences*, 22, 835–842
- Seifert, L. and Chollet, D. (2005). A new index of flat breaststroke propulsion: A comparison of elite men and women. *Journal of Sports Sciences*, 23, 309–320
- Sharp, B. (2004). *Acquiring Skill in Sport*. UK: Sports Dynamics.
- Stodden, D.F., Fleisig, G.S., McLean, S.P. and Andrews, J.R. (2005). Relationship of Biomechanical Factors to Baseball Pitching Velocity: Within Pitcher Variation. *Journal of Applied Biomechanics*, 21, 44-56
- Taylor, J., Mellalieu, S., James, N. and Shearer, D. (2008). The Influence of Match Location, Quality of Opposition, and Match Status on Technical Performance in Professional Association Football. *Journal of Sports Sciences,* 26, 885–895
- Tokeshi, J. (2003). *Kendo. Elements, Rules and Philosophy.* USA: University of Hawai'i Press.
- Tran, C.M. and Silverberg, L.M. (2008). Optimal release conditions for the free throw in men's basketball. *Journal of Sports Sciences*, 26(11), 1147–1155
- Tsuboi, S. and Imai, H. (1986). A comparison of successful and ill successful strikes and thrusts in the techniques of Kendo in relation to the speeds of shinais. On harai-men, men-kaeshi-do, debana-kote. *Bulletin of Institute of Health and Sport Sciences, University of Tsukuba (Ibaraki-ken),* [Online]. 71–78. Abstract from Ebsco Host Research Databases. Available from URL: http://web.ebscohost.com/ehost/detail?vid=10&hid=4&sid=f3dc1151-fc7e-4988-9f79-e0e50315e137%40sessionmgr7 [Cited 20-09-13].
- Ueda, F. (1985). On effectiveness of hitting and concerted actions between legs and arms in kendo: in the cases of men, kote and do hitting. *Bulletin of the Institute of Physical Education, Keio University (Yokohama, Japan),* [Online]. 25, 31–46. Abstract from Ebsco Host Research Databases. Available from URL: http://web.ebscohost.com/ehost/detail?vid=8&hid=4&sid=f3dc1151-fc7e-4988-9f79-e0e50315e137%40sessionmgr7 [Cited 13-10-13].
- Vodicar, J. and Jost, B. (2011). The Relationship Between Selected Kinematic Parameters and Length of Jumps of the Ski-Flying Competition. *Kinesiology*, 43, 74–81

A challenge for Tozando
By Donatella CASTELLI

I always found it strangely amusing, the fact that Japanese do not perceive exactly what "typically Japanese" is, for us "Gaikokujin". In fact, Westerners in general, even if they are more or less informed about the original features of Japanese culture (being it "popular" or "high"), have a clear perception of what looks and feels Japanese. For those who live and breathe Japan since they were in their mothers' wombs, the distinction could be paradoxically rather blurred.

In Japan, everything is Japanese, they would argue – the cultural landscape is amazingly uniform and everything foreign, that becomes adopted, is veiled by a Japanese patina, be it baseball, Italian cuisine or Jamaican rasta music.

So, how to find an unmistakably Japanese expression that would go well in styling a Kendo Bogu? After some considerable soul searching, I thought of choosing the classics – Hokusai's famous views of Mount Fuji. Not martial images, but recognizable and undoubtedly "typically Japanese".

So I threw the challenge to Tozando's craftsmen, to incorporate Hokusai's iconic Great Wave of Kanagawa (Kanagawa oki nami-ura (神奈川沖浪裏)) and the view of the Red Fuji (Gaifū kaisei (凱風快晴).

Not only did they accept the challenge, but they also successfully manufactured an amazing hand-stitched Bogu for me. I think that the result is stunning: the Great Wave has been reproduced in the Futon of Men and Kote and the Kazari ito has all the watery colors of the original ukiyo-e. The Red Fuji is reproduced on the Do Mune (not an easy task), while the Do Dai reminds the evanescent clouds. – yes, the Do as a whole may be flashy, but I think I can take a bit of flashy, in this old age.

What do you think?
And what would YOUR challenge be?

Tozando Custom-made Bogu
- What would your challenge be?

Made in Japan